PRIMAL FEAR

PRIMAL FEAR

Tribalism, Empathy *and* *the* Way Forward

✰✰✰

ROBERT M. SMITH

ISBN: 978-1-7372971-0-9
eISBN: 978-1-7372971-1-6
LCCN: 2021912783

Line editing, proofreading, cover design, and interior book design provided by Indigo: Editing, Design, and More.
- Line editor: Cooper Lee Bombardier
- Proofreaders: Kristen Hall-Geisler and Jennifer Kepler
- Cover & interior designer: Olivia Hammerman

www.indigoediting.com

*To my wife, Sally, and our three sons, Austen, Carson, and Ryan,
who are each blessed with a deep reservoir of empathy and the awareness
to use it in service to humankind.*

If I were God, I'd work on the reach of empathy.

—Frans de Waal, *The Age of Empathy*

Contents

Preface
A Pandemic Is a Terrible Thing to Waste
xi

Introduction
What Are We All So Afraid Of?
xv

Chapter One
Humanity's Story
1

Chapter Two
Modern Media and Ancient Bias
7

Chapter Three
My Children
29

Chapter Four
A Mirror Image
45

Chapter Five
Sit with Us
65

Chapter Six
Defusing Tribalism
77

Chapter Seven
Empathy Strikes Back
95

Chapter Eight
Head and Heart
107

Chapter Nine
Awareness to Action
117

Chapter Ten
Bridging the Divide
131

Acknowledgments
155

Bibliography
157

Preface

A Pandemic Is a Terrible Thing to Waste

Yes, COVID-19 was a brutal, unrelenting global pandemic. But it was much more than that. It was also a rigorous and unforgiving test of the health of our nation and its cultural, political, and operational wellness. And, prior to the introduction of a vaccine, America failed that test tragically—culminating in the sacking of the United States Capitol on January 6, 2021.

COVID-19 has revealed much, including the profound depth of our economic and social inequality, and has underscored the sorrowful loss of feeling as one nation, indivisible. During most major natural disasters—from hurricanes to floods to earthquakes and tornadoes—America has pulled together, with legions of volunteers laden with food and medical supplies arriving on the heels of our federal, state, and local government first responders. The president has flown in within hours of the tragedy, accompanied arm in arm by the governor and the local mayor.

We saw that unity during 9/11, not just at the World Trade Center, the Pentagon, or in Shanksville, Pennsylvania, but in every city and town across America. From many came one.

But not this time. Instead confusion, acrimony, and mixed messages were the currency of the realm. We acted more like Afghanistan than America: a delayed response, insufficient supplies, public denial, confused lines of authority, and most ugly and destructive of all, finger-pointing and hyper-partisanship. We acted tribally, with competing political and economic interests and unrelenting internal conflict.

Why, in the face of this horrific pandemic, did our nation fail to unite and answer the call, allowing COVID-19 to deepen our divisions, metastasize our smoldering intolerances, and fuel our tribal conflict? Literally tens of millions of Americans believed conspiracy theories that the pandemic was a hoax and the presidential election fraudulent, while armed demonstrators opposed virus mitigation efforts and medical face masks morphed into tribal flags.

The attack on the US Capitol, in an attempt to block the peaceful transfer of power following the 2020 elections, provided indelible evidence that America's divisiveness presented an existential threat to our democratic system.

Ironically, while these crises of trust in government and in one another reflect years of self-destructive national division, they also reveal the DNA of this social virus, the path to its cure, and the promise of a better day.

The DNA of our disease of national division is designed to attack the core belief that holds America together, our very motto: "Out of Many, One." As a result, we have become tribal—dividing into groups of the similar and like-minded, suspicious of those who are "different," and assuming the motives of the "others" are always malevolent as we retreat to the safety of our tribe, secure behind high walls of prejudice, suspicion, and echo chamber media.

This divisiveness corrodes the best that is America—our optimism, trust in each other, and capacity for collective action—hobbling the consensus we need to address the critical issues of our age, including economic inequality and climate change.

The conflict that we see today is rooted in fear that is hardwired in us, recently activated by a tsunami of disruptive change—global migration, economic dislocation, and social disruption. This rapid and accelerating change has activated three *primal* fears that are the products of evolutionary development in early human beings, traits designed to enable the survival of our species.

As I explain later in this book, my research into evolutionary biology, neuroscience, and political behavior identified those three primal fears as (1) the fear of others, (2) the fear of being left behind, and (3) the fear of social disruption.

To reverse this decades-long cycle of suspicion, animosity, and conflict, we must abandon many of our long and fiercely held political and cultural assumptions, take a brave look at the origins and anatomy of these primal fears, and consider who we are as human beings and as Americans.

Hope lies less with which leaders we choose or laws we pass; rather, it rests upon each of us as individuals questioning our own tribal biases and bridging tribal boundaries to better understand the "others" whom we see as different, even threatening.

This will require a bit more empathy from each of us. Fortuitously, a window into our empathy has been thrown open by two shocking recent events that I examine in later chapters: the killing of George Floyd and the attack on our nation's Capitol building on January 6.

Throughout this book I describe what I call the evolutionary interplay of fear and empathy, which has long shaped the course of humanity. This struggle between primal fear and our better angels is playing out in democracies across the world and is ridden with conflict. Some observers posit that democracy itself is at risk.

High stakes to be sure. But high stakes offer not only the chance for big losses but the chance for great opportunity as well. As the Black Plague prepared the ground for the cultural, political, and economic renaissance of Europe, perhaps amid the suffering from COVID-19 and decades of tribal conflict lie the seeds of a new day. If we learn.

I am hopeful that this book might play some small role in that learning.

Before the pandemic, I was working on a book about American hyper-partisanship. But COVID-19 helped me see America's conflict in a larger context with far greater implications—uncomfortable insight into who we are as human beings and how we got to this place.

This broader view has deeper roots than the pandemic's immediate cultural and political divisiveness—roots that subsume many decades of tribal conflict on familiar hot-button issues such as gun violence, immigration, climate change, racial injustice, and the ballooning socioeconomic inequity of the past few decades.

I have learned that only when we understand the common drivers of that growing political and cultural conflict, here and in other democracies around the world, will we be able to finally break the grip of this tribalism playing out every day on television, on social media, and in conversations with friends and family.

In this book I have traced the intricate connections that exist between the divisiveness we witness every day in America with modern tribalism, its evolutionary roots, and on to the small acts of empathy that could provide the antidote to this conflict. That antidote requires a great deal from each of us, including questioning our own tribal biases and the bridging of tribal boundaries to better understand the "others" whom we see as different, perhaps even threatening.

And that will require a bit more empathy from each of us.

Introduction

What Are We All So Afraid Of?

I am convinced that men hate each other because they fear each other. They fear each other because they don't know each other, and they don't know each other because they don't communicate with each other, and they don't communicate with each other because they are separated from each other.
—**Martin Luther King Jr.**[1]

The mass murder of innocents by a white supremacist in peaceful Christchurch, New Zealand, on March 15, 2019, provided undeniable proof that the growing global outbreak of social conflict, powered by fear and divisiveness, was metastasizing into a critical social pandemic—from which there is no safe place.

As if to ensure that we didn't miss the point, almost a year to the day after the Christchurch mass murder, a biological pandemic, COVID-19, went on a tear throughout the world, reminding us that as a global community, from some threats there is no safe place.

Ultimately COVID-19 will succumb to a vaccine, but what is the vaccine for the accelerating social divisiveness and conflict?

Even when COVID-19 passes, we will still live in an increasingly unstable world that threatens America and other liberal democracies across the globe. That threat emanates *not* from an adversarial nuclear

---

1   Martin Luther King Jr., "Address," Cornell College, Mount Vernon, Iowa, October 15, 1962, http://news.cornellcollege.edu/dr-martin-luther-kings-visit-to-cornell-college/.

power or a transnational terrorist group but from internal division and an open challenge at home and abroad to our democratic institutions and the rule of law.

Some say we have seen this all before; they are wrong. This is different.

I wrote this book because I was present when the seeds of America's tribalism were planted, and I soon became an expert witness to how the 24-hour news cycle and social media harvested that thriving crop of suspicion, fear, and conspiracy theories, all to the benefit of a new, less principled political class and their demagogic leaders. From a lifetime of leading three companies involved in political campaigns, issue politics, and corporate communications, I acquired a rare insight into the hyper-partisanship, extreme divisiveness, and even tribalism that we see in America today.

I was deeply immersed in many of the seismic social and political issues of our time: women's rights, social justice, gun violence, environmental protection, consumer rights, political reform, war, and more. I had a front-row seat to America's rich, recent history of political debate and competition as it unfolded over four decades.

Another reason to write about what I learned ringside over those years was the reluctant realization that I was an early, if unintentional, contributor to the political divisiveness that now haunts us all. So this book became a personal mission to find some answers for how this burgeoning snowball of suspicion, anger, and tribalism began and how we can stop it. I started with what I knew: the genesis of this hyper-partisanship.

During several decades as a pioneer of political microtargeting in politics and issue campaigns, I saw the early signs of these divisions: new analytics technology that grouped people by attitudes and beliefs; gerrymandered political districts that became unassailable to the "other" party; negative advertising targeted to likely believers; and an atomized, 24/7 news media with facts to fit anyone's conspiracy theory.

These tactical innovations enabled, perhaps even encouraged, *zero-sum game* legislative strategies (I win only if you lose), and a coarseness to our national discussion that too often smothered collaboration, compromise, and comity.

But how did we get here?

It is difficult to believe that it was only a few decades ago, in the 1950s and 1960s, that American teenagers decried America as too homogenous. Television shows like *The Adventures of Ozzie and Harriet* (1952–1966) and *Father Knows Best* (1954–1960), or the more recent retro of the age, *Mad Men* (2007–2015), reflected the ethos of conformity in dress, home decor, work decorum, and political views. But a mere two decades later, the tribalization of America was underway.

During most of my thirty-five years in politics and issue campaigns, extreme partisanship was rare and usually unproductive. So I never envisioned that hyper-partisanship, zero-sum politics, and fantastical thinking would become universally accepted in America. Our political system and social norms tended to drive voters to the middle. I believed that politics in our democracy would forever be characterized as the art of compromise.

I was wrong. And in retrospect, I can see how during the 1970s and 1980s my staff and I unintentionally prepared the way for a seismic shift in American politics. Long before Mark Zuckerberg imagined Facebook, we were pioneering ways to use data on American's purchasing behavior (from magazines to automobiles), surveyed attitudes and beliefs (e.g., on prayer in schools, abortion, and gun control), and personal residence and voting behavior to identify likely support or opposition to candidates and issues.

At the time, few took note of the true significance of this shift in the nature of both commercial and political communications: from mass to individual, passive to interactive. From our vantage point, focusing on consumer/voter interests and giving individuals a voice in government decision-making (letter-writing campaigns) and corporate governance (stockholder rights) was a positive—further democratizing communications and government.

In reaction to Watergate and "special interest" politics, we used that consumer and voter information for membership and fundraising appeals that helped transform small storefront organizations into major national reform and individual rights movements. In politics, this new grassroots clout meant that political novices and third-party candidates could now raise money, achieve name recognition, and conduct powerful get-out-the-vote efforts without big donor or traditional political party support.

At the time, it was heady stuff, and we thought of ourselves as the white hats. But soon campaign practitioners figured out that the merger of microtargeting and database technology meant that they could "preach to the choir" with precision, free of the risk that 50 percent of the recipients might be turned off by the content. This meant that candidates and their campaigns could put more of "an edge" on their messages—more partisan, more negative, more single-issue oriented, and less truthful. Few used the term at the time, but this was the beginning of modern tribal politics.

As the technology was changing, so were American attitudes and norms. The genie was out of the bottle, and the ground had been prepared for his arrival.

It did not take long before some candidates and single-issue organizations began to use this preaching to the choir technology to propagate explicit fear tactics and half-truths (e.g., Roe v. Wade is in imminent peril; the Democrats want to take your guns away). With this new approach, you could find those people most susceptible to your hard-nosed message, exclude those who might be offended, and use this diet of partisan exaggeration and fear to get "your people" agitated and mobilized.

With the turn of the millennium, broad adoption of the internet and social media became a game changer, expanding the power of microtargeting exponentially. No longer was the information on an individual's attitudes and beliefs inferential; now it was literal and no longer voluntary. It permitted the harvesting of vast amounts of information on tens of millions of people at the click of a mouse, at de minimis cost and at light speed, before anyone could yell "foul."

Years later, the full magnitude of the threat from this cynical trolling of fears and biases burst into view when the story broke that Russian military hackers were attempting to destabilize our elections using a microtargeting firm, Cambridge Analytica. A previously little-known database and political marketing firm, Cambridge Analytica harvested

vast amounts of data from individual Facebook users in areas identified as swing districts in the 2016 presidential contest. Their mission
was to undermine Hillary Clinton's appeal among working-class
voters and to boil the partisan pot.

Significantly, when these hackers masqueraded as legitimate
Facebook "friends," they often communicated their extremist views
to Facebook users with strong opposing views. In many instances the
Russians were not trolling to encourage support of Donald Trump;
rather, they used fake stories and conspiracy theories to incite anger
against Hillary Clinton. Too often fear trumps rational argument.
Insidious, but effective.

It was clear to me how the Russian hackers could, at least tactically, tip the scales in a close presidential election. Identify a small
but critical voter segment with sufficient grievances, in this case those
feeling disenfranchised from the political system, and then send them
messages that exploited an open wound. These messages were often
untrue but nearly always inflammatory. In 2016 that meant a targeted
voter segment of less than 100,000 voters in three to four states to
swing the election.

A clue to the Russians' longer-term objectives was their apparent
lack of interest in persuading but intense interest in inciting. Fear and
anger were the weapons they unleashed to undermine democracies
in over a dozen countries.

Still, the far more significant question, beyond how the Russians
could do it tactically, was why did a substantial percentage of
American voters enthusiastically embrace conspiracy theories that
tiptoed on the edge of violence? *Hillary Clinton is running a pedophile
ring in a Washington DC family pizza parlor.* That conspiracy theory
concerned a middle-aged man in North Carolina sufficiently that
he jumped in his truck and drove nearly three hundred miles up
to Washington with an AR-15 assault weapon to "break up the
ring." In the old days, we called this kind of behavior "crazy." Not
so anymore.

Of course, neither COVID-19 nor the Russians created the animosity between Republicans and Democrats or between scientists

and evangelicals; they merely exploited growing suspicion and anger to suit their strategy of exponential spread of misinformation.

Nevertheless, for this degree of issue absolutism and conspiracy theory acceptance to exist in a liberal democracy, a powerful emotional and psychological driver had to be at play. To be that successful, the Russians had to strike a raw nerve, something far more powerful than just partisan politics. In fact, Russian president Vladimir Putin and his GRU hackers had tapped into a vein of American voter anger and alienation more powerful than even their wildest expectations.[2]

They helped elect Donald Trump president, and they fanned the political tribalism taking root in America and in much of the Western world. Most significantly, they had found a strategy and supporting tactics that could destabilize democracies by exploiting their traditional strengths: freedom of speech; an open market of ideas; and a robust, unfettered media.

After months of research into Russian tactics and American reactions, and the enormous breadth and durability of this social and political conflict, I concluded that the evolutionary raw nerve that made this deception and divisiveness possible was deep-seated primal fear. The Russians were using modern technology to exploit ancient bias, and that was very frightening.

I soon hypothesized that the wellspring of this primal fear was modernity—a rapidly changing world increasingly defined by global immigration, accelerating technology, and economic dislocation. COVID-19 added confirmation to this hypothesis by placing an already-divided society under the extreme stress of a mysterious and deadly pandemic.

As I alluded to in the preface and elaborate in later chapters, scientific evidence suggests that from an evolutionary perspective, some fear is existential and primal. COVID-19 struck a primal nerve, further animating three preexisting American fears: of difference, of being left behind, and of rapid social change.

---

2   The GRU is Russia's military intelligence unit, formally known as the Main Directorate of the General Staff of the Armed Forces of the Russian Federation.

This hypothesis demands further research and explanation, so I begin this book seeking answers to three central questions:

What are we all so afraid of? Where does it originate? What is the antidote?

Two years of research into the evolutionary roots, neuroscience enablers, and social science solutions to this divisiveness followed, culminating in this book. In it I describe how this new targeting technology coupled with new media engages our fear centers; creates false realities; exploits our psychological biases; and finally, calls to action cohorts of angry, hyper-partisan followers—driven by fear so primal that it is impervious to counter-facts or -arguments.

Further, I explore how this primal, evolutionary fear is being exploited by opportunistic demagogues and autocratic leaders to challenge liberal democracy and the rule of law.

Fortunately, the story does not end there. I discovered a second, equally powerful evolutionary trait, also millions of years old, which seems designed as a counterweight to fear. That trait is empathy. Remarkably, as with fear, empathy is hardwired in the brain and is an age-old trait designed to aid human survival.

Integral to each of us but woefully underused, empathy could prove the most effective antidote to this tribal divisiveness if it is harnessed by our nations' leaders and by each of us individually. In that there is hope.

But first we need to better understand the difference between sympathy and empathy. Ironically, the tragic killing of George Floyd provides us with some painful but important insights to both. Sympathy is feelings of pity and sorrow for someone else's misfortune, an admirable and important emotion, but empathy is when you viscerally share the feelings of another. Empathy is walking in the other person's shoes. That is why empathy leads to action.

For an agonizing nine minutes and twenty-nine seconds, millions of Americans came horrifyingly close to walking in George Floyd's shoes. Within hours after police officer Derek Chauvin choked the last flicker of life out of George Floyd as he called for his mother, America changed forever. In the weeks after the killing, amid hundreds of national protest marches, people began to observe: "something has changed," "this feels different," "I'm optimistic that things will be different."

For people of color, the George Floyd killing was seminal and tragically familiar; for whites it was unique and terrifying. In that sense it was shared. Ironically, it became a unifying event.

Crucially, what we felt was not just more sympathy but something quite different: empathy on a grand and contagious scale. Accordingly, that difference between sympathy and empathy produced an uncommon and powerful reaction among white, middle-class Americans: *I get it: things must change.*

I believe that it was this visceral identification with George Floyd's suffering that led to the sense among so many of us that this time there will be change. Almost imperceptibly, the fight for racial justice had moved from defense to offense.

And that was not the only place where empathy was discovered. In the past few decades, neuroscience has discovered that empathy—putting oneself in another person's shoes—is activated by mirror neurons, hardwired in the same general area of the brain as is fear. Also, like fear, empathy is an ancient human trait, millions of years old, that has stood the test of time, serving the same essential purpose: the perpetuation of the human species. Empathy seems designed to be the counterforce to fear.

Empathy might appear a fuzzy, even ethereal antidote to the very insidious and contagious disease of fear. But like a vaccine for a biological or viral pandemic, empathy creates antibodies against fear's major enablers: ignorance and suspicion. By putting ourselves in the other person's shoes, we can better understand them and what makes them fearful.

When we were held captive by the video of George Floyd's death, our eyes sent a signal to a unique group of neurons in the prefrontal cortex of our brains, "mirror neurons" that allowed us to mirror, as best we could, the feelings of fear felt by George Floyd—almost as if we were each pinned underneath Officer Chauvin's knee. While white Americans might not have felt the breadth of fear born of hundreds of years of oppression, what they shared was an ancient, evolutionary fear of imminent death at the hands of a tribal foe. For most observers, previous exposures to television reports of civil rights violence remained mostly cerebral. This was different. For millions of white Americans, the cruel intimacy of that nine minutes and twenty-nine seconds overrode cerebral assumptions about race and criminal justice.

That might explain the role of empathy, but what was going on in the mind of police officer Derek Chauvin or in the minds of those who stormed the US Capitol? To answer that question, we need to broaden our focus from the actions of a few individuals to examine the broader world around us.

At no other time in human history has humanity faced a simultaneous convergence of three such massive waves of social change: the global migration of millions of souls across six continents; the acceleration of disruptive technology that displaces workers and challenges social norms; and a 24/7, interactive, customizable media often targeted to foment conflict by skilled demagogues eager to exploit it.

The result is a steady erosion of public faith in democratic institutions' abilities to keep us safe, preserve our rights and liberties, and sustain a society that reflects our values and ambitions. To many in America and across the world, these three social tsunamis have wreaked havoc on the pillars of social order.

Today just 19 percent of US millennials agree that a "military takeover is not legitimate in a democracy." Even among older Americans, 43 percent agree. In Europe, the numbers are 36 and 53 percent, respectively. Further, 25 percent of millennials believe that "choosing leaders through free elections is unimportant."[3]

How can Americans, who enjoy the fruits of history's most robust democracy, hold those views?

At one level this new cynicism toward democracy reflects several decades of extreme political divisiveness and hyper-partisanship. But the rise of extreme populism on the one hand and autocracy on the other suggests there is much more at play. The extreme

---

3   Yascha Mounk and Roberto Stefan Foa, "The Signs of Deconsolidation," *Journal of Democracy* 28, no. 1 (2017): 5–16.

divisiveness and absolutism that animates our new global discourse provides a clue as to its deeper origins.

The talk today is about profound differences in core values and wrenching divisions on matters too frequently described as "life and death." Those with whom we disagree are too often said to be "evil," harboring malevolent intent, and "totally wrong." Today debate is rarely enlightened by the facts, but more often mean-spirited and absolute in tone and content. There is little middle ground; choices are stark, and reason is in short supply.

Born of profoundly divergent reactions to this concurrent acceleration of change in demography, technology, and culture, this growing conflict has put enormous stress on the unifying fabric of our society—personal civility, political discourse, and respect for divergent views. Listening, understanding, and empathizing with "others" seems almost a thing of the past.

We appear to be connected by just one thing: fear.

Fear, and those who prey on it, seem in their ascendency: fear of terrorism, failed states and autocratic leaders, floods of refugees, growing economic inequality, and workers displaced by technology and rapidly shifting markets. In response, many have sought refuge in the familiar with "people like me," to the exclusion of those who are "different."

As I introduced very briefly in the preface, much of the world is experiencing social, political, and even military conflict that both drives and is driven by three great primal fears:

- *The fear of others:* danger from those of a different tribe—activated today by unprecedented global migration
- *The fear of being left behind:* losing the acceptance and protection of the group—activated today by economic inequality and social dislocation
- *The fear of social disruption:* losing the security of touchstones and traditions—activated today by culture-changing new technology, social media, and its concomitant impact on community values and norms

These fears are millions of years old, developed through evolution to help keep early humankind safe for the perpetuation of the species. But they have reemerged in modern times, inflamed by modern media, in response to this unprecedented economic and social change.

As a result, a new and particularly destructive form of tribalism is on the rise. We live in communities of the "like-minded"; seek out news media that reinforce our own biases; talk *at* each other, not *with* each other; and increasingly see the world as "them and us." This human condition is heartbreaking and advantages no one.

Most concerning, the discussion of how we got here tends to be superficial and distorted by the same tribal views that we seek to combat. Political extremism is not the cause of our divisiveness and distrust of one another; it is a symptom of something much bigger and more complex. Similarly, economic inequality is not the cause; while frightening, it, too, is a symptom of something even more alarming.

The face of America and the world is changing at light speed, and for many that change is terrifying. Here, too, COVID-19 did not give birth to that change, but it did deepen and accelerate it.

It is certainly true that change can be frightening, but that still does not explain what we see unfolding around us. Questions remain: What is driving this fear? What explains the existential nature to this fear? Why has that fear shut off listening and understanding those in the other tribe? Why are conspiracy theories and alternate facts on the rise? Why, after decades of a surge in popular governance, is democracy and the rule of law in retreat?

The desire to understand the root causes of how we got here, the implications to each of us and to the wider world, and what we can do about it led me on a journey that concluded with this book.

As you will see, I discovered that the genesis of the divisiveness we feel today is to be found in the evolutionary fear that was so essential to the survival of early humankind. Principally located in the amygdala (actually, amygdalae: there are two) close to the hippocampus, in the frontal portion of the temporal lobe of the brain, the amygdala "contributes to detection of threats and the control of body responses that help cope with the threat."[4]

The amygdala helps alert us to danger, too often manifesting itself as the fear of "others." While that fear response was essential to survival tens of thousands of years ago, I explain in this book how and why that fear of others has been so strongly activated in recent times, serving as the driving force behind what we now call modern tribalism.

Here is where the story gets interesting.

With the invention of magnetic resonance imaging (MRI), scientists were able to identify another evolutionary trait, also millions of years old, that appears to be heredity's balance to the fear of others: empathy. It, too, is a mature trait that has survived the test of time, residing in the cerebral cortex not far from the amygdala.

Empathy, which most of us take for granted, is an extremely complicated and powerful force in nearly all human beings—a force that science has only very recently begun to measure and understand. For centuries, a dozen major religions have described spiritual qualities that reflect empathy, and now science has found its presence and its mechanism within the human brain.

Nevertheless, empathy's evolutionary importance to the future of humankind, particularly at a time of growing fear of difference and resurgent tribalism, has yet to be fully appreciated. Understanding the biological roots of empathy, fear, and their interplay could prove central to making this a better world and perhaps to our very survival as a species.

In a sense, empathy seems to have evolved in humans to contest the destructive nature of another human trait: fear of people who are different from us. Interestingly, new research suggests that empathic feelings and fear of difference are both evident in young infants, even before they are socialized by family and culture.

Humans are hardwired with both seemingly contradictory emotions of fear and empathy. On the one hand, we might be fearful or

---

4   Joseph E. LeDoux, *The Emotional Brain: The Mysterious Underpinnings of Emotional Life* (New York: Simon & Schuster, 1996).

suspicious of immigrants, but when we get to know them as neighbors or coworkers, we can be open and generous toward them.

Reflecting upon the neuroscience and deep evolutionary roots of empathy within the context of how it plays out in everyday life—promoting better understanding and inspiring acts of altruism—we can begin to imagine the role that it could play in bridging divisions for the good of each of us, our communities, our nations, and our planet.

Equally important is how we, as a society and as individuals, can harness our empathy to tangibly change our world. While empathy may not be a magic panacea, it is a gift that humanity has possessed for millennia, awaiting our call.

As I have said before, this interplay between tribalism and empathy seems integral to humanity's story. The challenge is to overcome our primordial human impulses of fear of "difference" and embrace the better angels within each of us that insist we are all connected.

In this book I explore the convergence of science with the human experience. Together they explain the evolutionary causes of our current growing tribal fear. They also provide the hope that, if nurtured and well managed in enough of us, humanity's empathy could light the way forward to a world of less conflict and more understanding.

I have included stories of several seemingly ordinary people whose extraordinary empathy seems almost unimaginable, side by side with stories of everyday empathic acts of kindness and courtesy.

Lastly, I have concluded with two chapters about how each of us, as well as society's leaders, can harness our hardwired empathy to take specific, practical steps to reverse this global pandemic of fear and its resultant conflict.

Chapter One

Humanity's Story

It isn't that they can't see the solution.
It is that they can't see the problem.
—G. K. Chesterton[1]

One day a few years ago, Angela Cuozzo, a forty-nine-year-old from Albany, New York, decided to give one of her kidneys to a twenty-five-year-old woman from Bakersfield, California—a stranger. She had heard a poignant radio program on the shortage of available kidneys for patients whose lives hung on their getting a transplant.

So Angela went through the many months of preparation for the transfer, the surgery, and the subsequent recovery—all for someone she had never met.[2]

When a person donates a kidney to a desperately ill family member or close friend, we stand in awe of their act of altruism. We might even grapple with imagining ourselves making that sacrifice. The close connection between a donor and a family member provides us with some measure of understanding of the donor's motivations, perhaps even putting ourselves in that picture.

But what about the two-thousand-plus Americans like Angela who each year donate a kidney to a complete stranger? Who are they, and what motivates their profound generosity toward someone they have never met?

---

1   G. K. Chesterton, *The Scandal of Father Brown* (New York: Dodd, Mead, 1935).
2   Lenny Bernstein, "What Makes Someone Donate a Kidney to a Stranger?," *Washington Post*, April 28, 2017, https://www.washingtonpost.com/news/to-your-health/wp/2017/04/28/what-makes-people-donate-a-kidney-to-a-stranger/.

We might be inclined to place them in a category of iconic altruistic human beings like Mahatma Gandhi or Mother Teresa. But apparently they are just ordinary men and women by most standards: men, women, teachers, business people, blue-collar workers, young and middle-aged. Just folks.

With one outlier characteristic. According to research recently published in the journal *Nature Human Behaviour*, people who donate their organs to people not known to them do not view strangers as different or less deserving of support than family and acquaintances. They have less of the natural sense of distance from or suspicion of those outside their circle of family and friends.[3]

Does this rare sense of connection to strangers explain other extraordinary altruistic deeds and even everyday empathic acts of kindness and understanding? If so, what promise might this special connection hold for a world torn by tribal division?

These two questions have fascinated me for years. We understand why those drawn to certain professions, like priests or nurses, act for those in need; it is their training and their mission. Also, we have some understanding of the extraordinary bravery of soldiers who give their lives to save their buddies, people with whom they have a unique bond. Similarly, the selfless, heroic acts of parents who are driven by an almost instinctual need to protect their children are more easily explained.

But why do people help strangers, and how do we encourage more of it in ourselves and others? How might such acts, even the smallest everyday actions, transform our own lives, influence our communities, and even shape the larger world?

As I delved deeper into these questions, I discovered that there is a big story here, literally as old as humanity itself and right under our noses.

Recent research in evolutionary biology suggests that humans are hardwired at birth with two contradictory impulses: to be fearful

---

3   Kruti M. Vekaria, Kristin M. Brethel-Haurwitz, Elise M. Cardinale, Sarah A. Stoycos, and Abigail A. Marsh, "Social Discounting and Distance Perceptions in Costly Altruism," *Nature Human Behaviour* 1, no. 5 (2017), https://doi.org/10.1038/s41562-017-0100.

of people who are different from them, but also to feel empathy for people who are suffering. Complicating matters, it appears that those hardwired feelings of empathy can be conditional, too often restricted to "people like me"—those who belong to my "tribe."

We see this contradiction play out every day in the world around us. Refugees to Europe and the United States from war-torn countries in Africa are greeted by some who bandage their wounds, give them food, and find them shelter, while others jeer, turn their backs, or even assault them.

Some people see past the differences in race, ethnicity, and culture to actually "feel the pain" of the refugees as if it were their own pain; others, equally decent people, see refugees as so different as to be frightening, even dangerous, a threat to their way of life.

Why the disparate views?

Tests of newborns only a couple of months old, with very little socializing, reveal that they act both ways: crying out when they see other babies experiencing pain, but also drawing back, appearing fearful when they see babies of a different race or those acting "peculiarly."

Groundbreaking research in neuroscience, using MRIs to track brain activity, suggests all normally developed human beings feel empathy. When a diverse group of subjects looks at an array of photos of individuals—some of whom are experiencing pleasure and others discomfort—a distinct and consistent part of the brain lights up in the viewer's cerebral cortex, particularly when observing the photos of people in pain. Interestingly, convicted psychopaths show limited or no activity at all in the same part of the brain under the same conditions.

This new neuroscience research, combined with behavioral observations of infants and adults, appears to support the notion of an "empathy center" in most of us that responds to the sight of suffering among members of our human family.

Consistent with evolutionary design that favors characteristics that are likely to perpetuate the species, all humans and some other mammals have the capacity to regulate their empathy in response to perceived threats—dialing their feelings of empathy up or down depending on several criteria, including the risk to themselves if they act rashly.

Interestingly, fear can act as both a useful regulator of our empathy and a complete block. Those who shock us by their acts of cruelty appear to possess either damaged empathy or some psychological blocking mechanism, such as childhood experience, cultural training, or trauma.

Further, that blocking mechanism often involves three common elements: a greater-than-average fear of difference, a tendency to transform that fear into hatred, and a resort to tribalism as a refuge—seeking reaffirmation of their feelings from "people like me."

This struggle between our better angels and our fear of those not of our tribe, and how we cope with that struggle, seems fundamental to who we are as human beings. Today we see an acute resurgence of that struggle, in America and across the globe, as both real and perceived threats from new technology, globalization, and immigration drive people to tribal protection, to the exclusion of "others," and, too often, to violence.

The implications of all of this in our own lives, our families, communities, and the wider world are enormous. What role does this tribalism have in contemporary violence? How can we reduce the tendency to "other" people, to associate difference with threat and to then block our empathy? And how do we help others, from our global leaders to our next-door neighbors, find their empathy?

In a memorable scene from Harper Lee's American classic, *To Kill a Mockingbird*, lawyer Atticus Finch is standing on the jailhouse steps in front of an angry mob intent on lynching his Black client in 1940s Alabama. The scene takes place on a foreboding, dark night with a throng of hardscrabble farmers pressing in on Atticus.

Violence seems about to burst through when Atticus gets the unexpected help of his twelve-year-old daughter, Scout. Attracted to the torches that lit the night in the small town of Maycomb and fearing for her father, Scout confronts the mob. In the terms of a twelve-year-old, she reminds them that they are all from the same small community—of the same tribe.

She addresses the humanity lost in this faceless mob by addressing one man:

"Hey, Mr. Cunningham....Don't you remember me, Mr. Cunningham? I'm Jean Louise Finch. You brought us some hickory nuts one time, remember?...I go to school with Walter....He's your boy, ain't he? Ain't he, sir?"

Mr. Cunningham was moved to a faint nod. He did know me, after all.

"He's in my grade," I said, "and he does right well. He's a good boy," I added, "a real nice boy. We brought him home for dinner one time. Maybe he told you about me, I beat him up one time but he was real nice about it. Tell him hey for me, won't you?"

Scout reminds the men within this faceless mob that Atticus's fidelity to the law and concern for his Black client did not change the fact that he was still a friend and a neighbor. She further defuses the mob by putting a face and a name to it, creating a bridge of empathy for Atticus. So the mob—the impromptu tribe—slowly fades away into the night. It was a start.[4]

If we can map on an MRI the reaction of the brain to empathic feelings and demonstrate that acting upon those feelings is enormously rewarding to the individual who possesses them, can we capitalize on that knowledge and make empathy contagious?

History suggests that when we succeed in finding our empathy and turning it into even the smallest action, we enrich in profound ways both the world around us and our own lives. I invite you to follow the breadcrumbs with me to a world with less fear and more empathy.

But before we consider these individual acts of empathy and courage, examples that span decades, we need to stop for a moment to consider how today is different.

In this millennium, fear and its progeny, anger and conflict, seem more durable than in the past—seemingly immune to reason, even more absolutist and self-perpetuating in expression. The earmarks of this difference include the rise in conspiracy theories, fantastical thinking, and alternative facts.

---

4   Harper Lee, *To Kill a Mockingbird* (New York: HarperCollins, 1960), chap. 15.

A popular US television network, Fox News, was sued for trafficking in conspiracy theories that suggested that COVID-19 was a hoax manufactured by the Democrats to hurt Donald Trump's reelection.[5] Concurrently, armed protesters demonstrated against strict pandemic mitigation,[6] and the president advocated for the use of hydroxychloroquine for treatment of COVID-19, despite his health experts' warnings that it was ineffective and potentially dangerous.[7]

As I address later in the book, there are many reasons for today's climate of suspicion and division. But complicating matters enormously, and worthy of special attention from the beginning, is the toxic cocktail of ancient bias and modern media. Ancient bias, perpetuated by several age-old psychological human traits, has now been weaponized through modern media by those who profit from social disruption.

Never in history has humankind had to grapple with this explosive a combination, until now.

5   Bryan Sullivan, "Fox News Faces Lawsuit for Calling COVID-19 a 'Hoax,'" *Forbes*, April 10, 2020, https://www.forbes.com/sites/legalentertainment/2020/04/10/covid-19-lawsuit-against-fox-news/?sh=14e6e37f5739.
6   Lois Beckett, "Armed Protesters Demonstrate against COVID-19 Lockdown at Michigan Capitol," *Guardian*, April 20, 2020, https://www.theguardian.com/us-news/2020/apr/30/michigan-protests-coronavirus-lockdown-armed-capitol.
7   Jaimy Lee, "Hydroxychloroquine, Touted by Trump, Associated with Higher Risk of Death in Study," MarketWatch, May 22, 2020, https://www.marketwatch.com/story/hydroxychloroquine-touted-by-trump-associated-with-higher-risk-of-death-in-study-2020-05-22.

Chapter Two

Modern Media
and Ancient Bias

Facts are stubborn things; and whatever may be our wishes,
our inclinations, or the dictates of our passion, they cannot
alter the state of facts and evidence.
—John Adams[1]

During a *Meet the Press* interview shortly after Donald Trump's inauguration as president in 2017, counselor to the president Kellyanne Conway defended White House press secretary Sean Spicer's patently false statement about the attendance numbers at the inauguration by explaining that Spicer was using "alternative facts."[2]

The genie had escaped the bottle.

Alternative facts, conspiracy theories, subjective truth, reality TV, and relative reality are all terms that are shaping twenty-first-century information. And those polluted "facts" and customized "truth" are beginning to define who we are as Americans, what we stand for, and what we expect from the leaders of our society. So how did we get here?

In the 1950s, the centuries-old African American struggle for civil rights was transformed when television broadcast pictures of unarmed men, women, and children being beaten by police and

---

1   "Adams' Argument for the Defense: 3–4 December 1770," Founders Online, National Archives, https://founders.archives.gov/documents/Adams/05-03-02-0001-0004-0016.
2   Aaron Blake, "Kellyanne Conway's Legacy: The 'Alternative Facts'-ification of the GOP," *Washington Post*, August 24, 2020, https://www.washingtonpost.com/politics/2020/08/24/kellyanne-conways-legacy-alternative-facts-ification-gop/.

local toughs. A decade later, as graphic images of the brutality and futility of the Vietnam War flooded American homes, President Lyndon B. Johnson watched helplessly as the support for his war drained away.

The growing ubiquity of this powerful "new" communications medium made it nearly impossible for most Americans to remain unaware of these two human tragedies that might otherwise have remained at the periphery of our vision. That awareness engaged Americans' empathy at a speed and breadth perhaps unparalleled in our history and changed forever our nation's focus on race and our place in the world.

At the dawn of the new millennium, modern media in America and much of the world took an exponential leap into the unknown, with the proliferation of media channels made possible by new digital cable transmission, CNN's pioneering of the 24-hour news cycle, and of course, the harnessing of the power of the internet, particularly, in the form of social media.

The introduction of the smartphone delivered this new media on demand and on the go. Google made information available on nearly any subject to nearly everyone; YouTube allowed millions to use the impact of video to memorialize almost every moment, from the trivial to the tragic; Facebook permitted the creation of virtual communities; Twitter, text messaging; and Instagram gave birth to instant ad hoc groups of the like-minded. In many underdeveloped nations, handheld digital devices linked to social media permitted nations and small businesses to leapfrog costly communication in-frastructure in bringing buyer and seller together.

It was all fast, furious, and fragmented.

A full assessment of the impact of this change on both the volume and character of communication is still some years away, but it is already clear this technological progress has brought both blessings and burdens. It has transformed the nature of communication and the environment in which it exists. Families rarely gather anymore to "tune in" to a presidential address on the evening news; today infor-mation is "pushed" to us individually on our smartphones, computers, or as "breaking news" running across the bottom of our screen of choice during other programming.

We are also only now beginning to understand the impact that this new media is having on the social glue that binds societies and communities together, and how it impacts the human struggle between tribal behavior and empathic understanding. This is a complex subject with enormous implications, good and bad. It cries out for an informed, thoughtful, and candid national discussion.

Certainly communication plays a central role in understanding one another, particularly when it is an exchange between two willing listeners. It can also be used as a more one-sided exercise in selective listening or to cajole or intimidate. Much depends on the objectives of the communicators—listener and speaker.

Technological advancements in how we communicate, from the telegraph to radio and television, have extended communication's reach, speed, and persuasiveness. Modern media can now deliver messages in both image and sound in real time. As a result, it has transformed how people around the world select their leaders, how they learn of newsworthy events, and most importantly, how they perceive the changing nature of the world around them.

With a nightly blizzard of tweets to 85 million followers, Donald Trump has forever changed the power of the American presidency and transformed the rules and norms guiding political campaigns.

Outside of the world of politics, individual communication entrepreneurs have turned to social media to further charitable causes or publicize what they see as social injustice. Consider the summer of 2014, when two social media–driven trends spread quickly and powerfully. Beginning on Facebook, the Ice Bucket Challenge, a playful charitable appeal, spilled over into all popular media formats and captured America's imagination. Individuals could either donate funds to support ALS (amyotrophic lateral sclerosis) or dump a bucket of ice water over their heads. As anticipated, many people did both.

Celebrities, politicians, business leaders, and professional athletes were happily swept up in the cause in a matter of weeks. Before the fall season was in full swing, more than 17 million videos of smiling, drenched participants had been posted and shared world-wide. Awareness of ALS exploded, as did funding for this little-known but important charity. Google searches and page views of ALS sites spiked in response to the summer videos. Donations increased 300 percent within a one-month period.[3]

In decades past, there have been thousands of caring and clever charitable events that remained local and limited and only a few that have broken those boundaries, such as Jerry Lewis's annual global television special in the 1970s to raise millions for the treatment and cure of muscular dystrophy. But the Ice Bucket Challenge demonstrated how modern media can exponentially expand the reach and impact of altruistic events, creating a new self-propelled environment for social action and a new form of energy—contagious social awareness.

During a hot and humid August in 2014, the city of Ferguson, Missouri, became the site of nightly street protests in response to the fatal shooting of Black teenager Michael Brown by a local police officer. Here, too, photo and video images were instantly transmitted around the world, igniting a powerful force that elevated to mass awareness what might have remained a local incident. The developing clashes between protesters and police seemed to grow larger by the day, attracting demonstrators from other states and communities. Videos, photos, and stories of anger and violent confrontations spread rapidly, mostly organized on Twitter by the hashtag #Ferguson.

But unlike the Ice Bucket Challenge, there was nothing playful here: the demonstrators in Ferguson were profoundly serious about police violence, racial profiling, and decades of discrimination. In Ferguson, social media elevated the shooting of one man to the broader charge of police violence against Black people and delivered that message to a far wider world. The pain captured in the social media emanating from Ferguson was felt by millions around the country; or, as neuroscientists might say, the mirror neurons within

---

3   Lucy Townsend, "How Much Has the Ice Bucket Challenge Achieved?," *BBC News Magazine*, September 2, 2014, http://www.bbc.com/news/magazine-29013707.

millions of brains lit up as they also captured that pain, allowing people far from the city of Ferguson to understand its meaning.

In 2014, social media proved it could match television's powerful use of sound and image, and do so almost instantaneously, transmitted by thousands of eyewitnesses at the time and place of the "news." Most significantly, social media's unique quality of interactivity allowed for almost limitless contemporaneous comments on events as they unfolded, empowering people to shape the feelings and perspectives of others and even the unfolding of the events themselves.

However, for the Ferguson Police Department, social media was not a blessing; it robbed them of the initiative in controlling events in the streets and managing information about those events. As police around the world were rapidly discovering, the new media of the twenty-first century was decentralizing the control of information and, therefore, allowing others to define events and shape their outcomes before traditional authorities could act.

Again, in 2020, with the nation emotionally as dry as tinder after being locked in for almost two months by COVID-19, it burst into flames of outrage over the killing of African American George Floyd by a Minneapolis police officer. With 24/7 television and social media, the story and the video had spread worldwide in minutes.

Empathy for sufferers of ALS was ignited by the video messaging around the Ice Bucket Challenge, while altruism in the form of financial support was encouraged using text messaging and the internet. Yet latent, incendiary suspicion of police violence against African Americans became part of the broader American consciousness when social media ignited that suspicion following the killings of Michael Brown and George Floyd.[4]

Soon after the Ferguson demonstrations, social media lit up again, this time by angry comments and misunderstandings about both the purpose of the demonstrations and of the Black Lives Matter

4   Melissa Macaya, Mike Hayes, Fernando Alfonso III, Daniella Diaz, Jessie Yeung, Steve George, Ivana Kottasová, and Nick Thompson, "George Floyd Protests Spread Nationwide," CNN, last updated May 30, 2020, https://www.cnn.com/us/live-news/george-floyd-protest -updates-05-28-20/index.html.

movement. Some politicians, law enforcement officials, and media figures used the event to rally others in an opposing movement, "All Lives Matter." This was also new.

The tribal nature of this dispute was exposed by how both sides in the confrontation talked past each other, with little effort to listen to the other side, arguing about what attorneys refer to as "facts not in dispute"—revealing misunderstanding and fear on both sides. Social media had raised awareness and engaged some empathy, but it also reinforced tribal bias. These two global movements, the Ice Bucket Challenge and the Ferguson protests, provide important insight into the unique power of modern media to shape our society, in both connecting and dividing people.

Those movements demonstrate how that power can be used to increase our awareness and engage our empathy for others, but also to encourage suspicion, fear, and tribalism. Clearly, social media is a double-edged sword.

On a global level, the evidence that social media and the proliferation of media channels were decentralizing the control of information led some political scientists to speculate that more democratic media might lead to more democratic nations. Specifically, they hypothesized that in nations with autocratic regimes, democratizing of information could lead to the democratizing of governments. That hypothesis would be put to the test very soon and in profoundly different ways.

The massive 2011 public demonstrations in Cairo's Tahrir Square protesting the regime of President Hosni Mubarak of Egypt, coupled with parallel demonstrations in Libya and Tunisia, seemed to provide supporting evidence that democratic media begets democratic societies. These spring uprisings were powered by social media, directing citizens to the locations of growing demonstrations and alerting them to where the military and police were staging in hopes of smothering their dissent. Social media mobilized disenchanted citizens far faster than the police and military could react.

The same was true in Tunis and Tripoli. There, too, social media mobilized the empathy of millions around the world. Amid the YouTube videos and Twitter feeds, Americans, Europeans, and others in the Middle East could feel the poignant sense of hope that liberation was imminent. Empathy for their struggle grew with each day, and to Egyptians, Libyans, and Tunisians, this empathic support meant that they were not alone.

Soon governments fell in Egypt, Tunisia, and Libya, and this early digital uprising was giddily dubbed "the Arab Spring." To many observers around the world, these protests seemed an overpowering wave of inevitability and celebration: *this must be the right side of history.*

Alas, while social media could mobilize protests, it could not govern. Egypt has since returned to a military dictatorship and Libya to chaos. So far only Tunisia has evolved to a more democratic and inclusive form of government. In the absence of the iron hand of their former autocrats, Hosni Mubarak and Muammar Gaddafi, Egypt and Libya, respectively, reverted with a vengeance to their tribal fears, fomenting hatred and conflict between Islamists, local militias, and government militaries. The power of social media on display that spring in the Middle East was awe-inspiring, but it produced mixed results for democracy.

While new social media might be a powerful catalyst for democracy movements and can serve as a critical organizing tool, media alone cannot deliver a democratic government to replace a previously autocratic one.

However, in Egypt and elsewhere, social media produced some very encouraging, if unexpected, results. If used explicitly as an enabler of empathy, social media proved it can engage widespread openness to those we consider "others," promote understanding, and begin the process of breaking down tribal walls.

At least in the short term, social media appears better at democratizing the communication of ideas than it is at democratizing governments—better governance will take more time and greater effort. At the writing of this book, Turkey is going through a period of greater centralized government authority under President Recep Tayyip Erdoğan. Nevertheless, Gezi Park, in the heart of Istanbul, was the 2013 site of an unexpected and little-reported but remarkably uplifting example of social media enabling the bridging of divisions between some vehemently opposed groups.

In her book *Twitter and Tear Gas*, sociologist Zeynep Tufekci relates extraordinary first-person stories of how a combination of online and in-person communication produced lifesaving, consciousness-raising, and empathy-driven outcomes. This distinct communications combination, online and in-person, is key to fully understanding the positive power of social media.

The initial goals of the Gezi Park protest focused on environmental protection, safeguarding democratic expression, and maintaining safe places for vastly different social groups to gather. While it might not have been the protest organizers' original intention, social media brought people of divergent perspectives and beliefs together in Istanbul, face-to-face, which enabled them to connect personally.

The original design of the Gezi Park protest may simply have been to provide separate places for people of different backgrounds, ethnicities, sexual orientations, and political views to organize, but most human beings naturally seek connection, and that is what they achieved, crossing some daunting "no go" spaces. These common experiences and similar feelings helped push their differences aside and acted as a bridge across tribal divides.[5]

On January 21, 2017, the Women's March used social media to bring together millions of women of very diverse backgrounds in cities around the world to advocate for policies supporting human rights, women's rights, immigration reform, universal health care, reproductive rights, the environment, LGBTQ rights, racial equality, freedom of religion, and workers' rights. Like the Gezi Park protests, the Women's March produced many stories of people connecting eye-to-eye despite different religions, ethnicities, cultures, and political parties.[6]

While social media is not a magic wand of which a few waves can produce social and political change, it has proven very effective at bringing people together to permit conversations in search of better understanding and the bridging of differences.

---

5   Zeynep Tufekci, *Twitter and Tear Gas: The Power and Fragility of Networked Protest* (New Haven, CT: Yale University Press), 2017.

6   Women's Rights Organizers and Condé Nast, *Together We Rise: Behind the Scenes at the Protest Heard around the World* (New York: HarperCollins, 2018).

Further, the modern media story is far from over. Whether intended or not, inherent in the nature of that media is the unique capacity to alter the environment in which our societies evolve. It does this by engaging several basic human instincts, including fear and empathy, in powerful new ways—the same instincts that encourage both tribal exclusion and human understanding.

Therefore, it is important that we understand the human psychology that provides modern media with the fertile soil necessary for it to play such a unique role in how we receive, retain, and process information. For years, scientists have been aware of several psychological phenomena that distort how we communicate and receive information. I believe that this distortion explains much of the resurgence of both the ancient bias and tribalism that we see today.

One phenomenon is *perceptual bias*, which acts as an interpretive lens through which we receive and digest information. For example, if we believe that scientists and other experts are biased and seek to debunk beliefs that we hold dear, we are more likely to overlook even repeated recommendations on vaccinating against measles or quarantining and wearing face masks to protect against COVID-19.

In partisan politics, that perceptual bias is even greater, explaining why the same news story can produce very different conclusions from Republicans and Democrats about the same set of facts. So let's start there.

Professors Jennifer Jerit and Jason Barabas at Florida State University tested the notion of perceptual bias in politics in two clever ways. The first combined survey data with original media content analysis (the content of a news story versus what people recalled about the story), while the second reported the results of a randomized laboratory experiment.

They discovered that a voter's likelihood of remembering certain facts about government policy on trade, the federal budget, and the like went up by nearly a third if the policy was positively associated with the voter's own political party and declined by about a third if the policy was positively associated with the opposing political party. This degree of partisan perceptual bias among the subjects was similar whether the subjects were Republican or Democrat. Further, perceptual bias impacts memory. If news is positive about our political party, we are more likely to remember the pertinent facts than if it were a positive story about the opposing party.

No wonder today's political divisions make us wonder if both sides are working off of the same set of facts. Generally, it is the same set of facts, but not the same biases nor the same retention of positive facts about the other tribe. Perceptual bias interferes with our capacity to take note of or remember facts or information that we might consider inconvenient. The information is received; it simply doesn't stick.

Therefore, perceptual bias can serve as a subconscious means to avoid engaging our empathy when we fear that it might demand more of us than we desire to deliver. *I didn't stop to help because I didn't see the woman standing by her car with the hood up. When I talked with him, I didn't realize that he was so depressed. No one told me that she was sensitive about her weight.* While these examples are all very human, they reflect how perceptual bias can serve as an empathy-blocking mechanism that ill-serves humankind.

A close cousin of perceptual bias is *confirmation bias,* in which we look selectively for facts that support our preferred position, skipping over the inconvenient facts that challenge our view, often with no conscious awareness that we were even exposed to the alternative information.

In fact, our clever minds go searching for evidence that supports our current beliefs or perceptions; data that proves we were right all along. Like perceptual bias, confirmation bias is an empathy-blocking mechanism because it limits our awareness of the world around us, disadvantaging ourselves and our society.

Most worrisome, the research suggests that the more information we are exposed to on a partisan issue, the greater our bias. Jerit and Barabas summed it up this way: The result is a selective pattern of learning in which partisans have higher levels of knowledge for facts that confirm their worldview and lower levels of knowledge for facts that challenge them. This basic relationship is exaggerated on topics receiving high levels of media coverage.[7]

---

7   Jennifer Jerit and Jason Barabas, "Partisan Perceptual Bias and the Information Environment," *Journal of Politics* 74, no. 3 (July 2012): 672–84, https://doi.org/10.1017/s0022381612000187.

The third contributing psychological phenomenon is *motivated reasoning*, an emotional response that shapes how one might justify their perceptual and confirmation biases in the face of conflicting information. If dodging or selectively tuning out inconvenient information from the other tribe is insufficient, we use motivated reasoning as we might a corrupt umpire. Psychology Today describes motivated reasoning this way:

> Psychologists have had a field day in the past couple of decades demonstrating the many ways we deceive ourselves through our very processes of reasoning. While indeed our cognitive faculties are a distinguishing feature of humanity—they have lifted us out of caves and enabled all of the arts and sciences—they are also rooted in and subject to influence, or bias, by our emotions and deeply wired instincts. One of the most significant ways we warp our information processing and reasoning—and we do it outside of awareness that anything psychologically sneaky is going on—is called motivated reasoning....
>
> We engage in motivated reasoning as a way to avoid or lessen cognitive dissonance, the mental discomfort we experience when confronted by contradictory information, especially on matters that directly relate to our well-being.[8]

Motivated reasoning, which is often defensive, is designed to provide the intellectual justification for a point of view that is not necessarily supported by the evidence. We have all done this. During an animated dinner conversation with family or friends, we overstate our position on an issue, are challenged, and then scramble to not look foolish by resorting to specious logic.

When you combine perceptual bias or confirmation bias with motivated reasoning, you can get this kind of logic: *People say that the climate is warming because of human activity, and yet everyone knows*

---

8 "Motivated Reasoning," Psychology Today, accessed October 12, 2019, https://www
.psychologytoday.com/basics/motivated-reasoning.

that last year was the coldest winter in the United States in a decade. That is why I believe that climate change is a hoax. With perceptual or confirmation bias and motivated reasoning at work, it is possible that a person could make that statement despite having previously learned that last year's temperatures were anomalous to several decades of increasing temperature.

Some people may resist acknowledging that climate change is real because they fear the economic and lifestyle consequences from the changes necessary to fight climate change, while those in an opposing tribe may feel that they need to argue that every major storm is evidence of climate change. Tragically for our planet, the people who should be objectively discussing the implications of global warming and the imaginative solutions necessary to reduce its impact are retreating into the tribal comfort of their own perceptions.

So why do we deceive ourselves this way? The answer is central to understanding the resurgence of tribalism today and why it seems so intractable. It centers on a concept mentioned earlier—cognitive dissonance: "psychological conflict resulting from incongruous beliefs and attitudes held simultaneously."[9]

One thing that nearly all of us can agree on is that the twenty-first century has produced a deluge of information on almost every imaginable subject and that much of it challenges our societal traditions, customs, cultures, and rules.

The volume of information thrust upon us is literally too much to take in. Additionally, and critically, the information is often contradictory to what we were told previously and have believed for years. *Fat is no longer the diet problem; it is sugar. Bill Cosby is not the ideal father; he is a sexual predator. America does not have the best health care in the world, just the most expensive. Big cars are no longer symbols of success; they are symbols of excess.*

What we experience upon hearing this conflicting "new information" is cognitive dissonance, and it can prove to be very disruptive.

---

9   *Merriam-Webster*, s.v. "cognitive dissonance (n.)," accessed April 15, 2020, https://www.merriam-webster.com/dictionary/cognitive%20dissonance.

We human beings like consistency, for things to make sense and to be stable. But the modern world, amplified by modern media, is full of inconsistent, changing facts of enormous importance to people's lives: physical safety, job security, family health care, children's education, and on and on. For most people, these are "high stakes" matters.

When we are exposed to high-stakes cognitive dissonance, our minds resort to perceptual bias, confirmation bias, and motivated reasoning to bring a semblance of order to our world.

Of course, the problem with this human desire to avoid conflicting data and rules, particularly those governing our conduct, is that as a society we develop divergent perceptions of reality. As a result, we struggle to agree on a common set of facts to use in developing plans for collective action to meet a societal challenge or seize an opportunity.

Not surprisingly, democracy, with its emphasis on individual rights and universal participation, tends to highlight those differences, elevate divergent views of reality, and complicate agreement.

That is how cognitive dissonance plays a significant role in the formation of tribes (we are looking for consistency and familiarity of beliefs) and profoundly complicates understanding between tribes (we are exposed to the same facts but reach different conclusions). This global conflict between traditional norms and perceptions and modernity so evident today seems to have common roots in the cognitive dissonance created by accelerating social change.

Of course, social change is not new; it has been integral to human progress since humans harnessed the transformative technology of fire—altering forever the taste of woolly mammoth. What is novel today is the volume and speed of change, immensely complicated by a shrinking globe that has thrust humankind together, adding an infinite number of additional "differences" for humans to accommodate.

A recurring theme in this book is evolutionary fear—of others, of being left behind, and of social disruption—and the role that empathy might play in reducing fear and promoting better understanding. Modern media plays a complex role in all of this, particularly by magnifying the perceived cognitive dissonance that exists naturally during times of rapid change in traditions, norms, and ways of doing things.

Therefore, if we hope to reduce the divisiveness we see in America and across the globe, we will need to find ways to resolve the cognitive dissonance that has created so much uncertainty and fear to better enable our empathetic understanding of those who see the world differently.

This is no small task, according to professors Jerit and Barabas, who conclude: "Indeed, our results suggest that extraordinary levels of media coverage may be required for partisans to incorporate information that runs contrary to their political views."[10] So, persuading people that "the facts" suggest that their fears of "others," and the concomitant change that they bring, are unwarranted will require new strategies.

Further complicating matters, not only can modern media be misused to exploit our psychological weaknesses, but it can also be used to enhance those tricks that our minds play on our retention of facts and our perceptions of reality. There are three established theories about the nature of modern media, particularly television, which provide important insight into how modern media, cable, and social media could be compounding perceptual bias and motivated reasoning.

The first is *selective exposure*—the capacity of broadcasters, whether organizations or individuals (such as talk radio hosts), to target the similar and the like-minded for a series of common or related messages. It also allows individuals or groups of individuals to limit their exposure to selective messages, product offers, or points of view. Political media consultants and product advertisers have enthusiastically embraced this theory for years, targeting voters worried about immigrants from the Middle East, or consumers concerned about the whiteness of their teeth.

Selective exposure impacts not just politics but also social values and perceptions of who we are and how we should best live our lives, broadening its implications to society in ways large and small. This selectivity also works in reverse, as voters and consumers select media channels and personalities that agree with their perceptions

---

10 Jerit and Barabas, "Partisan Perceptual Bias."

and beliefs—strengthening perceptual biases and reducing exposure to contradictory views. The ultimate fulfillment of confirmation bias may be to select news outlets that report only what we want to believe is true. Presto: no cognitive dissonance!

The second is *cultivation theory*, about which University of California, Berkeley, communications professor George Gerbner suggests that the more one is exposed to a distorted or partisan representation of society, the more that person begins to believe that it represents reality. One could reasonably assume that this includes representation of race, culture, or partisanship.

As former KKK leader C. P. Ellis will describe in a later chapter, all of the stories and images to which he was exposed as a child supported what he was raised to believe, that "preferential treatment" of Black people was a chief source of the problems faced by poor white southerners. This notion of "preferential treatment" was often promoted by the white establishment to drive a wedge between Blacks and poor whites. Further, these distorted representations need not be supported by "facts," as we see in the creation and perpetuation of conspiracy theories.

For example, despite the exhaustive investigation by the Warren Commission into the assassination of President John F. Kennedy, there are intelligent, sane individuals who maintain that Lee Harvey Oswald did not act alone. I believe that they are struggling with the cognitive dissonance that a crime so extraordinary—assassinating the president of the United States, thwarting the power of the United States and presidential security measures—could not possibly have been carried out by a single, unhinged individual. For some people, a plethora of provocative movies, documentaries, and news media "special reports" all promoting conspiracy theories can provide an alternative reality that resolves the conflict.

A third theory about modern media posits a concept called *narcotizing dysfunction*, which contends that repeated media exposure to intense, graphic depictions of social situations such as war, natural disasters, or extreme poverty can desensitize the consumer to certain messages and lull them into a form of passivity.

One concern about narcotizing dysfunction is that it could lead to the feeling that because I watched the protest or witnessed the pain of the refugees, I need not take other action to help. *I am aware; therefore, I am engaged.* That narcotized failure to act might even involve the failure to apply our critical reasoning and core values to objecting to behavior we feel is immoral or out of line, so we just go along with it.

Some critics of President Trump's use of obscenities and untruths worry that the massive barrage of media around his controversial remarks could lead to desensitizing viewers and normalizing that behavior. Accepting this behavior as a "new normal" might include the unreflective assumption that people who are "different" (e.g., Muslims, immigrants, transgender individuals) merit greater suspicion and, therefore, represent a greater threat.

This is the tribal fear catechism: difference begets suspicion, suspicion begets threat, and threat begets conflict. A circular and self-fulfilling prescription for violence. So what does all this mean for the future of tribalism, empathy, and efforts to bridge divisions in our society and around the world?

First, these theories provide some foundational insight into why modern tribes of the like-minded form and why they are so difficult to defuse. The 24-hour news cycle delivers to homes around the world profoundly graphic and often sensational images and narratives of violence, cruelty, and corruption. As they say in the news business, "If it bleeds, it leads." This ubiquitous demand for titillating "news" not only encourages sensationalism among professional news outlets but also opens the gates to inaccurate or intentionally fraudulent news feeds with even lower standards of veracity and truth.

When we step back to consider the volume of destabilizing content that we twenty-first century human beings receive every day from hundreds of different media sources, it should come as no surprise that fears about one's personal security or place in society drive many to seek shelter in the age-old protection of tribes of people like me—from Baltimore to Baghdad.

Second, modern media, particularly interactive social media, has powerfully reinforced our sense of cognitive dissonance, which has increased the use of humankind's innate psychological release valves, including perceptual bias, confirmation bias, and motivated reasoning. It appears to be far more conflicting information than most people can process objectively.

Third, add selective exposure (seeking and being sought by like-minded media) and social media has assisted tribal recruitment through better targeting of future converts, strengthened the bonds of bias that tie tribal members together, and aid the reasoning necessary to justify suspicion, threat, and conflict. This applies to both ends of the political spectrum: *Terrorists are pouring across our southern border*, or *Nazism is growing in America like it did in 1930s Germany.*

Lastly, as research predicted, the enormous increase in the amount of information available to us today does *not* appear to have been particularly effective in breaking down entrenched partisan points of view.

Rather, what appears to be thriving within a new environment of intellectual and emotional segregation is fantastical thinking: "fake news," "alternative facts," and conspiracy theories. Fantastical thinking might be expressed this way: *No source of information can be completely trusted; therefore, it is only a "fact" if it sounds right to me.* Facts are available to support any worldview.

In sum, if tribalism is fueled by people with a perceptual bias toward a worldview that posits they are under attack, threatened, and aggrieved by people of difference and reinforced by selective, echo chamber media, we can now answer two questions so often asked by those on both sides of the partisan divide: Why do these people act this way? And why don't they understand that the facts don't support their view?

Given our built-in human biases, reinforced by modern media, what can we do to combat tribalism and encourage a more empathetic society? In the last two chapters, I propose an answer to that difficult question. But before leaving this subject of media's impact, let us conclude by addressing an intermediate question: What can we do to harness modern media's empathy-enabling qualities and diminish its supportive role in tribalism?

While partisan bias is difficult to reverse, there is at least one path that holds promise. The *Atlantic* writer Julie Beck, in an article on tribalism, noted another finding of Jerit's and Barabas's research that suggests we can reduce partisan bias if the source of the contrary information is someone from our own tribe: "While there's no erasing humans' tribal tendencies, muddying the waters of partisanship could make people more open to changing their minds. 'We know people are less biased if they see that policies are supported by a mix of people from each party.'"[11]

A dramatic example of how social media can be used to powerfully communicate such intratribal shifts in points of view involves a popular evangelical author and video star, Jen Hatmaker. She had a Facebook following of more than 700,000 individuals, a *New York Times* bestseller, an HGTV show, and the admiration and respect of predominantly conservative (theologically and politically) Christian women. She built her following through sharing personal stories about family, adoption, church, and conviction, enhanced by visuals of her home, children, and charitable work.

In 2016, she announced within her evangelical community a dramatic new point of view on the nature of homosexuality and the need for change within this group that in the past quarter century had increasingly defined itself in opposition to "the gay agenda." Hatmaker declared that LGBTQ individuals should be embraced and not pilloried. The immediate reaction against her was explosive, including significant financial consequences.

As expected, she was the target of hundreds of angry social media posts reflecting fear, hatred, and ignorance. For example, one person wrote, "I do not read anything by Jen Hatmaker anymore."[12]

However, there were other comments as well, different comments. Many women, both within and outside of the evangelical church, began dialogues among themselves via Facebook, asking questions and sharing personal stories. Slowly, but increasingly, women began

11 Julie Beck, "This Article Won't Change Your Mind," *Atlantic*, March 2017.
12 This comment was posted to Jen Hatmaker's Facebook profile on April 23, 2016.

to communicate their own progression of changed hearts and minds from shared personal experiences. Both "sides" wrote about uncertainty and pain, but also about empathy and understanding, as their need to cling to absolutist, tribal views began to dissolve.

- "It is truly helpful. I plan to use it when my wife's mom finds out in hopes that she won't disown our family."
- "While I may not agree with everything...There is nothing wrong with educating ourselves on these issues."
- "I believe that we can and should disagree and still love one another."
- "Can we model how to disagree with one another in a kind way? Why do so many disagreements end in hate? I think we all could [use] an extra dose of empathy."[13]

Similar stories on gay marriage and social acceptance have appeared in politics, including one from former vice president Richard Cheney, a stalwart of American social conservatism. He announced a change in his views on same-sex marriage when his daughter shared that she was a lesbian. His change of heart was followed by many others, some well known but most just people trying to grapple with their cognitive dissonance. Cheney's empathy for his daughter allowed him to walk in her shoes and reach a new understanding of people he had previously considered "different." Millions of Americans took note.

During this outpouring of announcements by well-known conservatives that their views on gay and lesbian rights had changed as a result of a better understanding that they acquired from family or friends, public opinion polls showed one of the fastest significant shifts in American public opinion on any social issue. Using opinion on same-sex marriage as the metric, the Pew Research Center reported this shift, particularly in views by those who had opposed it.

---

13 These comments were posted to Jen Hatmaker's Facebook profile on November 1, 2016.

Views on same-sex marriage have shifted dramatically in recent years. As recently as 2010, more Americans opposed (48%) than favored (42%) allowing gays and lesbians to marry legally. In the past year alone, support has increased seven percentage points: In March 2016, 55% favored same-sex marriage, while 37% were opposed.

The latest national survey by Pew Research Center, conducted June 8–18 [in 2017] among 2,504 adults finds striking increases in support for same-sex marriage among some demographic and partisan groups that, until recently, had broadly opposed it.[14]

So, changing the views of people deeply ensconced in tribes or tribal ideals is difficult but not impossible. Modern media may reinforce bias and fear, but it can also play a pivotal role in enhancing understanding by increasing awareness of the pain felt by others, engaging our empathy, and communicating diverse views among tribal members.

Twenty-first-century communication technology has forever altered the way we receive, send, and evaluate information. It has democratized the control of information, making it more difficult for autocrats to maintain a monopoly on facts, but it has also provided those same autocrats with a powerful electronic bully pulpit from which to provide "alternate facts." The new communication devices, channels, and interactivity have also changed how we connect with each other on a personal level, permitting us to be broadcasters of our personal news and anonymous critics of news about others.

While research on the effects of this rapid change in communication is still in its early stages, it is a reasonable hypothesis, based upon initial research and our own anecdotal evidence, that the misuse of modern media has had a significant impact on a resurgence of tribalism.

---

14 Pew Research Center, "Support for Same-Sex Marriage Grows, Even among Groups That Had Been Skeptical," June 26, 2017, http://www.people-press.org/2017/06/26 /support-for-same-sex-marriage-grows-even-among-groups-that-had-been-skeptical/.

The forensics of New Zealand's mass murderer Brenton Tarrant's computer showed he had been immersed in the activity and ideology of Anders Behring Breivik, the Norwegian right-wing extremist. Between the two of them, they took nearly 130 lives. Similarly, in the United States, the FBI has tracked the growing connection by social media of white supremacists' cells across the country.

Social media has been misused to magnify the fear that drives people to seek refuge in tribes of the like-minded. It has been misused to aid demagogues in creating and exploiting tribes of the suspicious and fearful who share common biases and grievances. It has been misused to direct those grievances toward convenient racial, ethnic, political, and other targets. And new media has been misused to unfairly discredit alternate opinions, open-mindedness, understanding, compromise, and worst of all, empathy.

Nevertheless, the potential of modern media, particularly social media, to also enhance our awareness of the world around us, engage our empathy, and promote altruism appears to be almost limitless. The key to a more empathic world is connectedness, and social media was born for that purpose.

Therefore, among the most significant contributions of social media may be its capacity to bring people together, including face-to-face, where greater understanding becomes possible when we discover our commonalities amid our differences. We must learn how to harness its highest purpose, human connectedness, and resist exploiting it to satisfy our lowest instincts, propagating suspicion, fear, and conflict.

Chapter Three

My Children

*I went to the woods because I wished to live deliberately,
to front only the essential facts of life, and see if I could
not learn what it had to teach, and not, when I came to die,
discover that I had not lived.*
—Henry David Thoreau[1]

As we grow older, it is only natural for us to wonder: What is the measure of our life? Well, in 1988, at the taping of the British television show *That's Life!*, Nicholas Winton received his measure in a dramatic way.

That's Life! had recently come across the story of Winton's rescue of 669 children from Nazi-occupied Czechoslovakia nearly fifty years earlier and invited him, now in his seventies, to sit in an audience of several hundred while his story was recounted in a video on his life.

It was the story about how Winton and his team organized the trains, obtained passage through Nazi Germany, finagled entry permits to Britain, and found foster families for hundreds of young children—right under the noses of the Nazis. When the lights came up in the studio at the conclusion of this remarkable tale, the host of the program, Esther Rantzen, surprised Winton and the audience with a question.

"Is there anyone in our audience tonight who owes their life to Nicholas Winton? If so, could you please stand up?" As one, the entire audience of over one hundred rose to their feet. Completely

---

1   Henry D. Thoreau, *Walden; or, Life in the Woods* (Mount Vernon, NY: Peter Pauper Press, 1954).

stunned, Winton wheeled around in his seat and cast his tear-filled eyes on three generations of the children he had saved during a dark time, long ago.[2]

It was a dramatic and well-earned accounting of a man's life. It is estimated that there are over six thousand people alive today because Nicholas Winton and his partner, Trevor Chadwick, put their busy lives on hold and at risk to save the lives of those kids. Is it possible that their echoes from a distant past could light the way forward for us today? I believe so.

Winton's story begins with the signing of the now infamous Munich Agreement by the major European powers on September 29, 1938, ceding the Sudetenland area of Czechoslovakia to Hitler in exchange for the German Führer's pledge to go no farther. It was hoped by many that the agreement would bring lasting peace, but it was clear to others that the Sudetenland was just the prelude to further Nazi aggression in Europe—with the balance of Czechoslovakia Hitler's next conquest.

In December of that year, Nicholas Winton, then a twenty-nine-year-old stockbroker in London, was looking forward to a ski trip over the Christmas holidays with an old school chum, Martin Blake. But on the twenty-second, a few days before he was to fly to Switzerland, Winton received a letter from Blake saying that he was in Prague, Czechoslovakia, not Switzerland, and Winton must join him there to see what he saw.

When Winton arrived in Prague, he found a city in chaos, over-flowing with refugees from the recently annexed Sudetenland: Jews, political dissidents, intellectuals, Romani—tens of thousands fleeing for their lives. This crush of refugees was dotted by thousands of young children trapped in Prague when Hitler denied their parents a path to freedom. Hitler had scores to settle and a timetable to keep.

It was an unimaginably heart-wrenching scene of desperate parents trying frantically to get their children out of Czechoslovakia and to

---

2 "Holocaust Hero Sir Nicholas Winton (That's Life – 1988)," February 9, 2021, video, 7:15, https://youtu.be/OqqbM1B-mPY.

safety, even if it meant never seeing them again. Winton was a well-read young man and, like most such people in Britain, Europe, and even in the United States, he was aware of the building refugee crisis in the wake of Nazi expansion. But seeing, hearing, and feeling it in person was a different experience.

On the ground in Prague, it was not a tidy picture of geopolitics, troop movements, or issues of national sovereignty; it was a scene of chaos—crying children, soldiers everywhere, and distraught parents sacrificing their futures with their young sons and daughters so that those they loved might have a future. Meanwhile, Nazi agents waited impatiently until Hitler could take the rest of Czechoslovakia and they could grab the lot.

Winton was deeply moved when he looked into the eyes of those frightened and confused children. Still, it is a long jump from sympathy for the plight of these refugees to putting his life on hold and at risk to take on what to most people would seem an impossible challenge. Back in London, a short plane ride away, he had safety, friends, family, a home, and a promising career.

In her excellent biography of her father, *If It's Not Impossible*, Barbara Winton posits that it was his values of fairness, kindness, and generosity, which he acquired from his childhood, that explain why he left his comfortable life to take up this extraordinary challenge for strangers.[3]

No doubt Winton's family instilled a sense of duty in him and the "right values." But that seems an insufficient explanation. Millions of people are raised with good values, yet they do not take off for another part of the world to rescue strangers from a distant danger that could so easily be justified as "not my affair." Only a very personal, deeply emotional experience or connection could command such a selfless act at this time and place.

Personal values, what we each hold dear, are developed over many years from individual experience, punishment and reward,

---

3   Barbara Winton, *If It's Not Impossible…: The Life of Sir Nicholas Winton* (Leicester, UK: Troubador, 2014).

the guidance of adult role models, and the shared values of the surrounding community. But Winton's reaction in Prague seemed more instinctive, emotional, and personal.

Winton lived a solid middle-class life in London, where most people felt that this refugee problem in Europe was someone else's business. Hadn't Neville Chamberlain, the British prime minister, given Nicholas all the excuse he might need to look away when he asked his countrymen the rhetorical question: "Why should we be involved in a quarrel in a faraway country between people of whom we know nothing?"[4]

Why, indeed.

Looking more closely, we see that Winton's awareness of the plight of the children was at a greater depth than that of most people in England and elsewhere around the world.

Chamberlain's faraway quarrel was anything but far away to Winton. The nature of his awareness of the refugee problem was different. His awareness went beyond the cold, cerebral facts of the situation, but included a depth of understanding of the pathos of the refuges; real lives were involved, and these people were not just refugees but men, women, and children. These were people just like his own family, with similar hopes and dreams and loving relationships.

His reaction included both a cerebral analysis and an emotional insight, a powerful combination. Viewing it this way, Winton understood that the children's situation was dire and that the fate of these children was *his* business, an urgent business.

After arriving in Prague where he could see the pathos of the children firsthand, his awareness began to transform into a very personal, empathic identification with the children at risk. Winton adopted their plight as if it were his own. Soon he began calling them "my children."

That transition from "those refugees" to "my children" is the magic of empathy and the promise it holds for us today—feeling what the other person feels.

---

4   BBC Archives: Chamberlain addresses the nation on peace negotiations, https://www.bbc
    .co.uk/archive/chamberlain-addresses-the-nation-on-his-negotiations-for-peace/zjrjgwx,
    accessed April 12, 2019.

Perhaps it was the anti-Semitic bullying he suffered as a child. Shortly after he arrived in Britain as a young boy, his parents changed their family name from Wertheim to Winton and raised Nicholas as a Christian in the hope for a better fit in their new homeland. He was bullied nonetheless. Or perhaps it was his feelings of statelessness when he and his family arrived in Britain from Germany, which aided his understanding of how these children felt as refugees.

Whatever the full explanation, Winton had put himself into the tiny shoes of those young Czechoslovakian children: alone, confused, and terrified. Once inside those shoes, Winton was hooked. No longer was the danger the exclusive, sole province of these kids from a different land; Winton felt the danger as if it were his own. Their trauma became his trauma.

But he was also able to manage that trauma and stay focused on the complex challenge of doing something about it.

Winton adopted the plight of these children as a danger to himself, but he did not lose himself in that empathy. Rather, he maintained his perspective about the magnitude of the crisis and was able to call on his skills as an organizer and advocate to focus on the best way to use his limited time and resources to save the maximum number of children.

When the Czechoslovakian borders were closed and his Kindertransport was ended, he understood that he had done all that he could do, so he returned to London to pick up his life where he left off. During those months in Prague, Winton demonstrated that he possessed empathy's special connection with his fellow human beings but also the cerebral competence to manage the power of his empathy to productive effect. He did not let his feelings of empathy overpower him; rather, he translated that empathy into practical action.

This capacity to maintain practical perspective on what is possible and channel our empathy for the most useful impact is crucial to harnessing empathy's power for good.

Winton's empathy went toe to toe with the Nazi Party, perhaps modern history's worst example of tribal fear and violence, and he won. While outmatched, Winton changed the lives of thousands.

While he regretted that he was unable to save all the children and their parents as well, he went on to pursue a full life that included a successful career, a family of his own, and not surprisingly, considerable charitable work. He continued to channel his active empathy into altruism toward others, which enriched his own life as well as the world around him.

Particularly fascinating was Nicholas Winton's rare depth of awareness of a situation that was publicized for all to see, but which was dismissed by most as "not my business." This deliberate awareness of the world around him, near and far away, was essential to activating his rare understanding and intense identification with these refugees from a different country, culture, and language.

I have borrowed the word *deliberate* from Henry David Thoreau's *Walden Pond* to empathize the unique quality of conscious awareness of the world around us: "I went to the woods because I wished to live deliberately, to front only the essential facts of life."[5]

Deliberate awareness means seeing our surroundings in a way that pierces the fog of our daily habits, putting aside our smartphone to listen closely to a friend's problem. It awakens us from the insensate state that guides us past the homeless woman without seeing and challenges the justifications we use to avoid getting involved in something that requires more time or courage than we feel we have at hand.

In Winton and others who perform exceptional acts of empathy-driven altruism, this rare commitment to living life deliberately aware of the world around them is central to who they are as human beings. For Winton, it was first his awareness of the developing Holocaust that led him to Prague and then his very personal awareness of the plight of those refugee children that engaged his empathy.

We should not lose sight of the less central but still essential role that Martin Blake played in saving those kids. It was his awareness of the children's plight that led him to direct Winton to meet him in Prague to see what he saw and feel what he felt. In fact, the original act of altruism that preserved the lives of those 669 children was

---

5   Thoreau, *Walden*.

simply a letter from Blake to Winton asking him to cancel the ski trip and come to Prague. A small act of empathetic concern with profound impact.

With Winton's empathy committed, he was able to feel the suffering of the children as if it were his own. Feeling what the other person is feeling is the very definition of empathy: "The ability to understand another person's feelings, experience, etc."[6]

Yet there is an important distinction here. Literally feeling what the other person feels isn't sympathy, which is good and important, but is one step removed, more at a distance: *I am sympathetic to the cause of the Syrian refugees, and to help them I give money to Doctors Without Borders.* This is an example of sympathy, an admirable reaction that reflects concern and caring.

Nevertheless, sympathy is distinct from empathy in that it is most often a cerebral reaction: *We cannot permit this type of suffering in the world; it is so unfair.* This reaction often originates from a sense of injustice, which is also admirable but plays out more as a considered, cognitive reaction rather than the emotional response that is empathy.

As I noted earlier, sympathy is experiencing feelings of pity and sorrow for someone else's misfortune, an admirable and important emotion; but empathy is when you viscerally share the feelings of another. Empathy is walking in the other person's shoes. Walking in their shoes does not mean you adopt their full identity for even a moment, but rather you feel a sudden emotion like fear or excitement as they do. When the football player incurs a severe, blindside hit in reaching for a pass, fans grimace, even jump back, as if they were the intended target of the hit. For a split second, they were in his cleats.

Let me be clear, my intention is not to belittle sympathy, which is critical to a humane society, but rather to highlight the uniquely powerful qualities of empathy.

To expand on the football analogy above, empathy is adopting the emotion—feeling the terror of an infant amid the dust of the

---

6   *Oxford Learners' Dictionaries*, s.v. "empathy (n.)," https://www.oxfordlearnersdictionaries
.com/us/definition/english/empathy?q=empathy.

bombed-out building by putting yourself in the place of the Syrian child covered in blood, buried in rubble. Less dramatic, perhaps, empathy is also feeling the pain, humiliation, and loneliness of the high school girl taunted for not fitting in, or the exhausted, despairing man fighting for his personal dignity in the unemployment line.

So, empathy is putting oneself in the other person's shoes and walking around a bit.

Another important difference between sympathy and empathy is that empathy breaks through more cultural and attitudinal barriers to understand "others"—from refugees to people of different political views. Empathy elicits more than "feeling sorry" for someone; it encourages us to understand what the other human being is experiencing.

For example, you have an acquaintance who holds different opinions than do you on an incendiary issue like abortion, so when you are with the acquaintance, you usually stay clear of the subject. It becomes a wall between you. Then one day she shares with you her very touching personal story on the subject. It is a very human story that makes you feel her intense pain and confusion on the issue, so gradually you begin to understand why she holds those views. You might even conclude, *While it might not change my views on this issue, I understand why she feels so strongly, and she has given me something I need to think about.* It is a start, a connection with another human being that might otherwise have been lost. It is a bridge.

Empathy can break through strongly held biases about the intention and character of those who hold views different from yours. That type of insight often requires more than an intellectual exchange to consider what you share with this person and how you are connected, to avoid "othering" them and retreating to the safety of your own tribe. This help in understanding the other person and in bridging differences may be the greatest gift of empathy.

At those moments we can feel what the other person feels, almost as if we were inside their skin. Empathy is also present when we experience that feeling in the pit of our stomachs when we nervously watch the acrobat perform on a tightrope one hundred feet above us. Or the reflexive groan we make when the college football player collides head-on with another player. Or the tears we shed at the news story of the mother who lost her child. These empathic feelings come from a deeper place and can be more revealing than a cerebral exchange.

As you will see in later chapters, empathy is a quality within each of us that is both hardwired by evolution and something that can be nurtured and developed. But most importantly, empathy is less about feeling sorry for the other guy and more about connecting with the other guy.

But where do these feelings of empathy come from, and why do some people act on those feelings while others turn away? If we look more closely at the case of Nicholas Winton, we see that he had developed four qualities that enabled his empathy and led him to act on what he felt.

As I noted earlier, the first quality is *deliberate awareness* of the children's suffering, eyes and mind open to what was happening in the time and space around him. The second is *empathy* itself, feeling the children's suffering as if it were his own.

There are two important additional qualities reflected in Winton's altruism: cognitive *perspective* to resist both the fears that threaten empathy and the danger of losing his own identity in his feelings for others, and *altruism* itself, the action that was driven by his empathic feelings.

Perspective is where the cerebral activity fits in. You decide that you must do something to help the homeless man, and your reason does two seemingly contradictory things: it helps you determine whether helping the man might endanger yourself but also helps you set aside latent prejudices that might create fear where fear need not exist. *When that man waved to me for help with directions, I hesitated because he looked confused and disheveled. But when I paused to look a little closer, I realized that he was just lost, as I have been many times, and needed my help.*

If you see a person in pain, your empathy might lead you to adopt that pain as your own, while your reason searches for perspective to protect you and manage your fear. With the support of your perspective, you have both the commitment to act and the green light to go ahead, which is where altruism comes in.

In her biography of her father, Barbara Winton describes his childhood as a German émigré, which created personal challenges for fitting in, but being from a different land also produced a worldview, an interest in and sense of affinity for a world beyond his new home in Britain.

Certainly that worldview contributed to Winton's awareness of the crisis building in 1938 Europe and made it seem less "foreign" and more "his business." So his awareness of the plight of the Czechoslovakian children was not just serendipitous; it was made possible by his personal commitment to be knowledgeable about the world around him and to take seriously the pleadings of Martin Blake, who alerted him to the unfolding crisis.

That deliberate awareness brought Winton to Prague, where he found his empathy.

Importantly, while Winton was certainly central to this rescue mission, he was not alone. He had two partners, each of whom showed all four of those elements key to engaging and harnessing empathy for good. Trevor Chadwick, a teacher at a school in Dorset, and Doreen Warriner, an academic and leader in the British Committee for Refugees from Czechoslovakia, found the courage to run toward the crisis and not away, to fully embrace their native empathy, which enabled their altruism.

When you examine how the intrepid threesome encouraged and steadied one another during the trying months in Prague, you begin to wonder if empathy could be contagious.

Trevor had come to Prague to adopt two of the refugee children on behalf of his school, but seeing firsthand the magnitude of the tragedy unfolding, he stayed until Hitler invaded Poland and the Czech borders were closed.

Doreen was on her way to the United States to begin a Rockefeller Fellowship she had just recently been awarded, but she chose to forsake the safe and comfortable halls of academia to rescue people the Nazis had singled out for being different and, therefore, dangerous.

The key to Nazism was to persuade Germans, Austrians, and others that these people—Jews, Romani, the handicapped, the mentally ill—were different, not the Aryan ideal, and thus a threat. This threat necessitated banding together in an impenetrable Aryan tribe to protect its members and resist this growing diversity. Their tribal rituals, massive torchlight rallies, extravagant parades, the burning of books, and trumped-up charges of criminal conduct all increased their tribal members' incipient fear of what those strangers might do, which eventually devolved into hatred and violence.

In organizing this complex rescue mission in Czechoslovakia, Winton, Chadwick, and Warriner were, in a sense, pitting their empathy against the Nazi-inspired tribal hatred for "others." Their actions championed the belief that we are all connected and share a common humanity, while the Nazis' brutality divided Jews from gentiles, Romani from the middle class, and children from their parents.

The three Brits worked tirelessly together and in parallel. Followed by Nazi agents and never sure when the borders would close for good, they worked under extraordinary pressure to pull off a small miracle with meager funds and only limited cooperation from any other country. Most Americans and Europeans were able to look away and justify inaction, seemingly unaware of the impending human crisis. But not Winton, Chadwick, and Warriner.

All three were ordinary in terms of upbringing and career choices but extraordinary in the decisions they made on behalf of others in need. While also very different individuals, the three were connected by their shared awareness of the crisis that brought them to Prague, the empathic connection that they felt for the refugees, their courage to face the threat with the refugees, and the conviction to act.

When Winton looked out at that crowded train station with those hundreds of frightened kids and their frantic parents, at some emotional level he felt that he was one of those kids—he saw the chaos through a child's eye, he heard the frantic screams and the parents' panic as could only a child. A parent knows well that feeling of longing in the pit of their stomach when they drop their child off for the first day of school or summer camp, because the parent is adopting their child's feelings of loss and uncertainty.

This is how putting yourself in another's shoes unleashes a powerful force. An extraordinary force for good.

After a week in Prague, Winton, Chadwick, and Warriner could not just hop on a plane back to the safety of home in England, leaving those kids to Nazi death camps. If they left the children, in a sense they would themselves be left behind. They had to act—their empathy demanded it. All three made themselves open to the refugees' suffering and adopted their fear as their own. So they did the only thing that they could do—they responded with extraordinary acts of courage and generosity.

But if empathy is in all of us, why do some people find their empathy and act on it, while others do not? A brief look at the history of humankind's uneven relationship with empathy helps explain why.

Since the ancient Greeks, the study of empathy has mostly been the province of philosophers until the last few decades when serious scientific investigation began. Those who studied the origins of empathy viewed it as a cognitive function, a rational calculation. The plight of others was something reasonable humans observed, evaluated, and then decided whether to act upon what they observed. *If I help him out, I can expect him to do something for me.*

For the longest time, those who studied what they then called "sympathy" and only later "empathy" and resultant acts of "altruism" viewed them as strictly calculated responses, motivated by hopes of receiving something of equal or greater value in return. That return could be social recognition for "doing good" in this life, or even in the next one. This cognitive view dominated the conventional explanation of empathy and altruism through most of the twentieth century, despite abundant anecdotal evidence that this response included a strong emotional component: *I felt so badly for them; I felt that I had to do something.*

But this earlier view did not explain those selfless acts for which there was no evident self-interest involved. Not surprisingly, some concluded that altruism must be a random genetic mutation, an outlier in the long progression of human evolution. What good was empathy in furthering the human species, it was reasoned, if it was likely to expose a person to danger—falling behind to help a wounded comrade with the enemy in hot pursuit? As rational beings, why would we give of our wealth or even risk our lives for another unless we had something to gain?

To that way of thinking, the ledger of life's actions must be balanced.

Also, not surprisingly, most early studies of empathy concluded that it existed exclusively in humans, who are reasoning beings. But spoiling that convenient, human-centric view, over the past few decades, scientists have begun to suspect that empathy might also exist in other mammals such as apes, elephants, and dolphins. Observations of dolphins creating a protective ring around shipwreck survivors to ward off shark attacks, elephants leading a blind member of the herd day after day, dogs sitting by their sick or injured masters for months, or bonobos tending the wounds of other apes have intrigued scientists for years.

Frans de Waal, a Dutch biologist, one of the world's leading primatologists and former director of the Living Links Center just outside Atlanta, Georgia, made his life work the study of how primates think and feel. It was largely because of his disciplined scientific approach to understanding how and why mammals (primates in particular) feel empathy and demonstrate altruism that de Waal was named one of *Time* magazine's one hundred most influential people in 2007.

His remarkable work in understanding primates and other mammals has extraordinary implications for our understanding of humans as well. De Waal's description of altruism in mammals is an insightful bridge to humans: "Mammals have what I call an 'altruistic impulse' in that they respond to signs of distress in others and feel an urge to improve their situation."[7] He reached this conclusion through painstaking observations of apes, elephants, and dolphins who, like us, are all mammals, give birth to live young, and crucially have the capacity to sense suffering or distress in other animals and the impulse to take altruistic action to help.

De Waal's conclusions were in defiance of nearly all the prior scientific assumptions that empathy (the driver of altruism) was a cognitive skill, something entirely taking place in the brain's cerebral

---

7   Frans De Waal, *The Bonobo and the Atheist: In Search of Humanism among the Primates* (New York: W. W. Norton, 2013), chap. 2.

cortex where self-interest could be weighed against altruistic sacrifice. This cognition model assumed humans and primates do not "feel" the suffering or distress of another of their species through some empathic emotional response, but rather, more coolly observe the distress and make risk-reward calculations before responding.

This self-interest motivation is commonly espoused to justify acts of extreme selfishness among humans. Famously, Gordon Gekko, the lead character and heartless corporate raider in the popular film *Wall Street* (modeled after the real-life corporate raider Ivan Boesky), argued that "greed is good." Good, ostensibly, because it incentivizes hard work and wealth creation, which lifts the entire economy. Further, as the argument goes, much of that wealth creation ends in philanthropy, the product of "calculated altruism," or contributions made to the local charity in exchange for social recognition and business connections.

These somewhat cynical assumptions about the origins of human motivations were encouraged by behavioral scientists such as B. F. Skinner, economists such as Milton Friedman, and many public policy advocates of a rational behaviorist model of human conduct. If you want people to buy houses, give charitable contributions, or eat healthier food, you provide intrinsic positive incentives like price discounts or negative incentives like additional taxes on sugary soft drinks.

This school of thought suggests that there is no such thing as genuinely altruistic behavior that emanates from an internal emotional response inspired by feelings of empathy for another's suffering. All such actions are risk and reward calculations guided by learned behaviors from past actions.

Ironically, our growing understanding of the powerful motivations in humans, beyond reward and punishment, was significantly advanced by studies of primates and the work done by de Waal and his colleagues. De Waal describes a study done at Taï National Park in Côte d'Ivoire, in which chimpanzees came to the aid of others in their group who had been wounded by leopards. These "altruistic" chimps "licked their mates' [wounds], carefully removed dirt, and waved away flies that came near the wounds. They protected injured companions and slowed down during travel in order to accommodate them."[8]

Some of de Waal's studies took years to conclusively prove that the actions of their chimpanzee subjects were genuine signs of empathy and not just trained behavior in search of a reward. Over many months, de Waal and primatologist Victoria Horner developed a method to neutralize reward and punishment training and isolate behavior in chimpanzees that appeared to definitively demonstrate that apes have emotional empathy and concomitant altruism.

Using plastic tokens of different colors and wire mesh separating two chimps, they gave one chimp both red and green tokens. If the one chimp chose a red token, only she received a food reward; if she chose a green token, both she and the chimp behind the mesh received a reward. Quickly both chimps figured out the significance of the different tokens. The chimp who received the tokens had no incentive to pick the "generous green" over the "selfish red," but she did. Over time, she responded to the pleas of the other chimp and began to pick the "generous green token" two out of three times.

The significance of evidence like this that mammals possess an innate sense of empathy for others suggests many things, including that empathy is not likely a recent evolutionary development or genetic experiment but rather a long-standing, well-developed, mature, and fully tested trait.

This is a trait with a purpose, one that has stood the test of time in other mammals as well as humans.

De Waal argues that if evidence of empathy were restricted to the frontal lobes of the brain, which developed more recently, that would suggest that empathy was a young, experimental trait. But as we will see later, science has established that empathy plays a much more significant role. That evidence appears to confirm de Waal's view that "empathy is part of a heritage as ancient as the mammalian line. Empathy engages brain areas that are more than a hundred million years old."[9]

---

8 Frans De Waal, *The Age of Empathy: Nature's Lessons for a Kinder Society* (New York: Penguin Random House, 2009), chap. 1.
9 De Waal, *Age of Empathy*, chap. 7.

While the proof of empathy in animals was derived initially only in observational studies, it was enough to challenge the conventional belief that empathy is strictly a cognitive, learned skill actualized for the individual primate's self-interest. Rather, these studies showed that empathy is far more "simple and automatic."[10]

This first step was a breakthrough for animal science and inevitably raised the question of whether the empathy and altruism we see manifested in humans is from the same emotional impulse seen in other mammals. From here, the hunt for the nature of empathy got extremely interesting.

If there is a unique brain process that produces an "altruistic response" in primates who share 95 to 98 percent of our DNA, then we know where to look in humans to learn about empathy in each of us. Extraordinary acts of selfless courage and generosity by "ordinary" people like Nicholas Winton led philosophers and scientists alike to finally ask the essential first question in understanding empathy: If not for their self-interest, whatever possessed them to risk so much for complete strangers?

As I explain later, modern science revealed a powerful truth about empathy: it has far more to do with connection than cognition and exists as an opposite pole to evolutionary fear that creates suspicion, distrust, and distance.

The preponderance of modern scientific inquiry seems to suggest that empathy provides a critical balance to fear. That is why I believe that within a better understanding of empathy lies hope for the future.

---

10 Frans de Waal, *Primates and Philosophers: How Morality Evolved* (Princeton, NJ: Princeton University Press, 2009), 41.

Chapter Four

A Mirror Image

*Sometimes you have to say goodbye to the things you know
and hello to the things you don't.*
—William Faulkner[1]

On November 7, 1959, John Howard Griffin walked out the door of his hotel and into the bright sunlight of a beautiful New Orleans fall day. Less than a week before, he had entered as a white man; now he exited as a Black man. Thus began one of the most remarkable personal odysseys of modern times.

Griffin traveled to New Orleans from his home in the small Texas town of Mansfield in search of something that has forever challenged humanity—understanding the other guy. With the backdrop of the growing tension of the American civil rights movement in the late 1950s, Griffin, an accomplished writer, was seeking an answer to why there had been a recent national spike in suicides by Blacks but not among whites.

He was animated by far more than just this statistical anomaly; he wanted an answer to what he believed lay behind the data: Why do some human beings treat others with such immense cruelty to body and soul as to drive them to take their own lives?

Griffin was driven to understand how a Black person's despair could be so deep that he cared not whether he lived or died. On that fall day in 1959, he knew only that part of the answer must lie within the cruel segregation and humiliating Jim Crow laws that

1   William Faulkner, *A Fable* (New York: Penguin Random House, 1954).

pockmarked America's Deep South. But why did courteous, church-going, family-oriented whites allow, even participate in, such treatment of other human beings?

Sixty years ago, John Howard Griffin was on the path to understanding a very subtle quality to tribal fear and its corrosive impact on both those who are reacting in fear and those that are the object of their fear.

He knew from his years as a journalist in the South that if a white man were to ask a Black man a penetrating question about racial hatred and injustice, he was likely to get the answer Blacks learned over three centuries of oppression, the safe answer: "Things are just fine." And to ask those same questions of a white man, particularly in the South, was to find him hewing to a well-rehearsed tribal line: "We have wonderful, harmonious relations with our negroes."

But Griffin wanted the truth.

Further, he sought not what these people, white and Black, said they were feeling; he wanted to feel it himself. Although there was not much helpful research on empathy or tribalism at the time, Griffin understood at some level that the answers to these questions, which had eluded most Americans for so long, could only be found in the depth of the personal experiences of the Blacks and whites who lived it day to day.

Even the growing number of news reports on race relations and his own interviews of Blacks and whites did not reveal the truth. He needed to feel what Black people feel, literally.

In the tradition of the earliest medicine, Griffin chose to use his own body and mind as the test subject. So, for a week, with the help of a New Orleans dermatologist, Griffin took high doses of a drug used to treat vitiligo, a rare disease that created bright white patches on a person's skin. The drug dramatically darkened his skin and, to magnify the effects of the drug, he lay under a sunlamp for hours to soak up intense amounts of ultraviolet rays.

In a week he no longer recognized the strange and somewhat frightening man staring back at him in the mirror. That man was a Black man, as surely as any he had ever seen.

Despite some disquiet about what lay ahead, he felt ready to begin his journey by bus through America's Deep South. He traveled under his own name and told the truth about his professional and educational background. The only thing that he changed was his skin color. That was enough.

He may have been the same man inside, but for everyone else he became a repository for their perceptions and prejudices toward Blacks. For nearly two months he was taunted, threatened, and required to ride in the back of buses, while being turned down for jobs for which he would have been accepted in an instant as a white man. Most startling to him, however, was the profound indignity he suffered as the target of white people's tribal "hate stare" if he raised his eyes to theirs.

Somehow, being different, being black in skin color, was enough to generate hatred from people he did not know, people to whom he had not spoken a single word. Griffin got what he was looking for, an in-your-face journey through the belly of race-based tribalism.

He rode the segregated buses across Louisiana, Alabama, and Mississippi, terminating his odyssey in Atlanta, Georgia. When he arrived in a Mississippi town in which the lynching of Black teenager Emmett Till for allegedly flirting with a white girl was still raw, he traded furtive and fearful glances with other Blacks on the bus. Without anyone saying a word, the Blacks aboard understood that they must wait for the whites to exit first. Nor was an objection raised about Blacks being required to walk a quarter of a mile to the "colored" restroom. The story of the lynching was all the instruction anyone required.

Griffin spent many stressful hours and very full days with dozens of Blacks and whites, but none saw through his disguise. He used the "colored" restaurants, bathrooms, hotels, bus waiting rooms, bars, drugstores, and soda counters. A few times when he mistakenly found himself in a white area, he was nearly always quickly straightened out by willing white volunteers. Once, exhausted after a long walk, he stopped to rest on a public park bench when a seemingly benign older white man walked over and made it clear that he was in the wrong place: "You'd better find yourself someplace else to rest."[2]

---

2   Griffin, *Black Like Me*, 41.

Universally, the Blacks with whom he met during his journey clearly understood, at the deepest level of human feeling, the challenges he faced. To those he encountered in America's Deep South, he was a Black man—for whom all assumed rights manifested in the US Constitution were suspended.

Over many trying days and nights—often living with the most impoverished Blacks, sharing their food, their work, their companionship, and even their beds—he found that these mostly dirt-poor folks were universally generous to him, no matter how meager their resources. They were brothers and he felt the connection.

He was now part of their tribe, delineated by skin color and bound together by the shared experience of exclusion and the cruel whip of discrimination.

They talked of the indignity, humiliation, and frustration that came from being blocked at every turn when trying to rise up, only to be ridiculed with comments like, "See that, colored people are poor and uneducated because they just don't have the ability to get ahead like white people."[3]

Griffin quickly learned that the Blacks who put him up in their homes, often little more than sharecropper shacks, were not looking to be repaid for their kindnesses. Repayment was not necessary because they shared a special connection with Griffin and an understanding of the pain that he faced because of his skin color.

Despite all his efforts to become Black, Griffin still could not fully share with southern Blacks the disabling pain and humiliation that is derived from generations of slavery and prejudice. Nevertheless, his skin color admitted him to a new tribe and gave him a remarkable insight into how different the world looked through the eyes of a member. While empathy, as in all things, has its limits, it can open our eyes to the world around us, and what we do with that may well be limitless.

This is what Griffin had come for, what it felt like to live as a Black man in America's Deep South. But he also learned a great deal about another tribe: southern white segregationists. Here he

---

3   This is my illustration.

discovered subtle tribal conduct defined by local mores and unspoken assumptions. This unstated tribal conduct was by necessity revealed to southern Blacks to "keep them in their place"—within their own tribe of subjugates. At the same time, these subtle cues were often hidden from northern whites who "wouldn't understand." But Griffin saw them unfiltered as a Black man.

He had conversations with white men and women in which he learned of the indirect ways that otherwise friendly, hospitable whites justified their treatment of Blacks in the 1950s. The lubricating justification that eased their consciences and kept their empathy at bay required unquestioning belief in two convenient myths handed down from generation to generation:

1. Blacks are not as bright, ambitious, or capable as white people; they are fundamentally "different."
2. Given their intellectual and cultural limitations, most Blacks are happy with their lives of subservience to paternalistic whites.

Clearly, the world looked quite different through the eyes of a member of the tribe of southern white segregationists. The contrast between white and Black "realities" was stunning to Griffin.

When it came to Blacks, white southerners in the 1950s used an intellectual, emotional, and ultimately political construct developed over generations to blind their innate powers of awareness and hold their natural empathy at bay. It was not that southerners were bereft of such feelings for their fellow men and women; their kindnesses and courtesies to fellow whites are legendary. Yet they had relegated Black people to an alien tribe, inherently different from them and potentially dangerous.

That "othering" of Blacks was sufficient to obscure the abundance of contradictory facts that challenged the white racial dictum, making it extremely difficult or irrelevant for whites to even imagine walking a mile in the shoes of a Black person. As a result, simple kindnesses and acts of altruism between tribes were far too rare.

Even small acts of generosity between tribes came with the risk of social excoriation, even violence, from other members of their own tribes. So the walls of tribal exclusion and animosity were rarely breached. Had Griffin's secret crossover between tribes been revealed, he would surely have been in serious physical danger.

Understanding this made Griffin appreciate even more those heroic acts of whites, in both the North and the South, whose awareness of this systemic bias and discrimination activated their empathy and led them to defy their tribe's segregationist norms in courageous acts of altruism—from the time of slavery through to today.

There are countless stories of southern men and women who risked their standing in their communities, and in some cases their lives, smuggling Black slaves to freedom in the nineteenth century and standing shoulder to shoulder with Blacks at civil rights marches in Selma, Montgomery, and Birmingham in the twentieth. For several hundred years, empathic Americans of goodwill have worked tirelessly and with great courage to bridge the tribal walls of race in our country to be rewarded by only limited success.

Sadly, that courageous, tribe-bridging empathy was far too rare and often severely punished by those fearful that any breach of their tribal walls would "change everything."

So how do some people manage to maintain their focus on the unpleasant truth about the world around them to find the will to defy the tug of tribal suspicions and fear, so that they might better understand the feelings of those who live outside their tribe?

Griffin felt the pain, humiliation, and growing despair of being "othered" in America's South in the 1950s. Of course, this was the purpose of his journey. However, it was his exceptional awareness of southern whites' behavior that gave him important additional insights into how their subtle tribal behavior both enforced Jim Crow and salved their consciences.

Being the object of their suspicion and bigotry gave Griffin a rare insight into how "othering" Blacks had, ironically, also created fear within whites. To white segregationists, Blacks were different, resentful, threatening, and the subject of much mythology, particularly regarding sexual prowess.

The exclusion of Black people from white society reduced aware-ness and familiarity and bred fear, which often tipped over into anger, hatred, and even violence. White racial myths became real to southern segregationists, imprisoning them in a world that narrowed their own lives and creating its own vicious circle—fear begets discrimination, discrimination begets fear.

This was an important insight about not just southern whites but also so many other seemingly well-intentioned individuals who unknowingly trap themselves within tribal beliefs and norms, limiting their worlds, as they are increasingly consumed by their own fears. It is epidemic in our modern world as religious, cultural, and ethnic tribes lash out at "others" as their worlds close in on them.

Ironically, modern technological advances such as jet travel and the internet, which for many have made our global community seem more connected, brought with them visions of a very different world that to some is very threatening in its difference—driving them back into tribes of the familiar and the like-minded, separating much of the world into "them and us."

To white America in the Deep South of the 1950s, that threat in-volved integration with people of a different racial tribe. Today the threat felt by many Americans across the country is integration with people of a variety of different tribes—racial, ethnic, cultural, and political.

Therefore, the recent increase in activity by white supremacists, ultra-nationalists, and nativists should not surprise us, as the accel-erating social and economic change of the twenty-first century has, for some, intensified a terrifying sense that tribes of "others" are becoming the majority, displacing the incumbent majority.

While this evolutionary fear is gradually dissipating in humanity worldwide, for many the speed of change is outpacing the speed of adaption.

Griffin returned home to Mansfield, Texas, to write the story of his journey, *Black Like Me*, which became an international bestseller. But returning home also exposed him to virulent hatred from people in his hometown and around much of the country. How dare he impersonate a Black man? He had broken the code that had preserved an uneasy and profoundly inequitable "peace" in America's South.

He refused to flee his Texas roots despite months of death threats. It was his home too. These people were his friends and neighbors. Yet many of those friends and neighbors were from a decidedly different social tribe than Griffin.

Griffin did not wear a distinctive uniform or follow alien rituals but attended the same church and patronized the same restaurants as those who felt threatened by him. They were set apart from Griffin tribally by differing attitudes toward Black people.

So, while driving on a country road near his home, Griffin was rewarded for his loyalty to Mansfield by being stopped and beaten with chains by a group of white toughs who left him for dead. He survived and went on to write several more books on what he had learned and to become a unique and powerful voice of the civil rights movement of the 1960s.

Griffin said that he was motivated to risk body and soul to understand better what Black Americans felt deep down, in the very fiber of their beings, after generations of oppression and humiliation. And it allowed him to see firsthand the subtle but mind destroying discrimination that so many whites claimed did not exist in the South. But one insight that he unearthed was even more profound. Perhaps his greatest observation was a more generalized one.

As tragic as the treatment of Blacks in America has been for centuries, it is but one product of a worldwide, age-old human trait that threatens us to this day. While we may be endowed with the evolutionary instinct of empathy, we are also burdened with an opposing instinct of fear and distrust of difference.

Regional social norms, family upbringing, superstition, and cherry-picked religious precepts can combine to create a complicated web of prejudice and denial that make much more difficult the acceptance of "difference."

I chose to recount John Howard Griffin's extraordinary act of personal courage literally walking miles in another person's shoes because his journey provides unique insights into the building of informal yet powerful tribes. And how decent, well-meaning people can be drawn into those tribes without conscious awareness of the damage tribal conflict can inflict on our social cohesiveness. Those that possess the whip hand often fail to see that the lash also falls hard on themselves, their friends, and their families.

Since Griffin's journey, these tribal divisions have mutated and metastasized throughout America's political system—turning partisan preferences into tribal suspicion and hatred. Now the "othering" of people of difference has expanded beyond race, ethnicity, and religion to include political affiliation, partisan ideology, and views on any number of single hot-button issues.

I use the word *metastasized* deliberately. This new tribal fear mimics cancer, spreading rapidly to all of society's organs with uncontrolled growth, feeding off the environment it inhabits.

In 1960, just a year after Griffin's social experiment, survey research revealed that only 5 percent of Republicans and 4 percent of Democrats would be unhappy if their son or daughter married someone of the opposing political party. By 2010 that partisan bigotry and fear jumped to 50 percent of Republicans and over 30 percent of Democrats.[4]

Most worrisome, in 2016 the Pew Research Center reported that a full 45 percent of Republican voters and 41 percent of Democratic voters felt that the policies of the opposing party represented a threat to our nation. In just over fifty years, America's political parties, which had been admired for their moderation and effective compromise by democracies around the world, had become warring tribes.[5]

It is no wonder that the representatives of those parties in the US Congress are stalemated in a zero-sum game of tribal partisanship— *I can only succeed if my opponent fails*—fighting over issues too frequently called matters of "life or death."

The damage to our government's effectiveness and our society's comity from this new political tribalism is incalculable. While the self-defeating nature of this partisan tribalism might be evident to

---

4   Pew Research Center, *Partisanship and Political Animosity in 2016*, June 22, 2016, https://www.pewresearch.org/politics/2016/06/22/appendix-a-measures-and-scales/.

5   Pew Research Center, *Partisanship and Political Animosity in 2016*.

most Americans, we seem unable to resist cheering on our tribe and denigrating, often threatening, those members of the opposing tribe. American politics increasingly reflects mob psychology—talk show hosts egging on their followers with conspiracy theories and unsubstantiated claims about political opponents.

Just as segregation was a self-defeating social contract for America's South—whites' fear of Blacks kept the destructive wheels turning for centuries—today we are turning those wheels again and far more broadly to include partisanship, ethnicity, national origin, and religion. So, too, is today's growing tribalism a self-defeating social contract. A nation divided by tribal walls cannot stand.

Further, while there is much gnashing of teeth about the symptoms of the problem and much blame for the "other guys," there is very little discussion of the root causes of this national corrosiveness, acceptance of a share of the blame, or efforts to understand the other side.

Voters blame "the politicians" (but rarely their own politicians), while the politicians blame each other. Few political leaders and few voters are pausing their partisan attacks to ask, What has caused this mean-spiritedness, this adversarial approach on nearly every issue, and why am *I* now acting this way?

Again, like the segregated South, in Congress and state governments there are very few leaders with the courage to challenge their own tribe to demand that we work with the other political party to discover the real causes of the problem or to find real solutions.

As of the writing of this book, there are early signs that some in American politics are growing weary of the combat and reflecting on a day of far greater political comity. There is also some discussion of how economic upheaval may be partly responsible for many of the angriest voters but no awareness of the underlying, primal causes of this anger.

Fewer still are connecting the dots between the evolutionary fear, the extraordinary social disruption, and the rise of tribal conflict—in America and across the globe. These forces are sufficiently large enough in scale and emotional intensity to awaken some of our worst evolutionary instincts. Left unaddressed is the connection between this partisan animosity and the disruptive changes that have swept like a wrecking ball through the lives of Americans over the past fifty years.

Rapidly accelerating disruptive technology and globalization of trade and immigration have benefited many consumers through lower prices, more consumer choice, and more diverse communities. But for many others it has led to economic hardship and social disruption. The face of America has changed in ways that more and more citizens find frightening.

Civilization's natural moderation of our evolutionary fear of difference has been overwhelmed by the speed of change.

As I described in chapter one, accelerating this centrifugal force driving apart American society and the societies of many other nations is the recent fragmentation of the media into an almost limitless number of sources of information. This increased competition for the attention of American consumers and voters has encouraged the media to be increasingly sensational, often intentionally shocking, while providing a false sense of security in the confirmation of their partisan points of view in tailored echo chambers—unalloyed by factual shades of gray or serious alternative opinions.

As the old saying goes, "Even paranoids have real enemies." But a growing number of media outlets needlessly frighten people and then convince them that they were right to feel scared—a virtuous cycle of increased ratings and revenue. This has led to what today is called fantastical thinking, the willing suspension of disbelief to reaffirm the conspiracy theories and alternative facts that provide some order in a seemingly disorderly world. This media virtuous cycle has helped create a social vicious cycle, changing America in frightening ways, reinforcing evolutionary fears of difference as we withdraw to tribes of the like-minded.

Here, too, we are ignoring Griffin's insights from over a half century ago. Myths about Black citizens were central to keeping the segregationist tribe huddled together. Today it is "alternative facts" and "fake news" that insulate the fearful and angry from awareness of the true makeup and intentions of the other tribe, even of the world around them.

If we step back even further to broaden our perspective to our world community, nation-states are themselves increasingly resembling opposing tribes, some with weapons of mass destruction. As a result, the risk to humanity grows.

Further, when those tribal nation-states are whipsawed by their polarizing voters and special interests, it becomes harder for the world to come together to act on critical issues such as climate change, economic inequality, or the plight of refugees.

Central to the writing of this book was the question, If fear of difference is a centrifugal force driving us apart, is there an opposite, centripetal force that could pull us together?

As I have noted earlier, there is a ray of hope amid this complex new reality in the growing scientific and academic understanding that empathy could be a direct counterforce, one that naturally encourages better understanding of each other, and which could lead to bridging those divides.

Despite enormous skepticism today, the desire to understand the other person remains a foundational human trait, essential to the successful development of social bonds. It is a desire that resides in all of us, even if dormant in many. How can we hope for a loving family without understanding each other? How can a city or town be a community, a business better satisfy its customers' needs, or a government be responsive to its voters without understanding the feelings of others?

Anyone who has been blessed with a successful marriage or business partnership or has played on a sports team has learned that understanding their partner's emotional needs is essential to working, playing, and living together. This understanding of our fellow human beings is essential to social interaction—and to our survival as a species.

But given the tribal state of the world today, it would be reasonable to ask, Is this innate desire of humans to understand the other guy just the fantasy of the determined optimist, or is it real, something that we can put to practical use in healing our divisions?

To answer this question, it is useful to look at the science of empathy.

How we understand the feelings or emotions of others has intrigued and eluded the scientific community for centuries, partly because there has never been a means to track and quantitatively measure emotions beyond observing how they are expressed. We often say that emotions reside in the heart, but most of us know that while that is an appealing romantic notion, serious scientific investigation into emotions is centered in the brain.

But where in the brain does this understanding of the feelings of others originate, and what is the process of activation? If empathy is truly a powerful evolutionary trait, it must be driven by the brain. To find the answer, we must travel to Parma, Italy, the city that gave the world Parmesan cheese.

There, in 1993, a group of scientists discovered almost by accident the answers to how we feel what others feel. This time Parma gave us a discovery that many in the scientific community considered as significant to psychology as DNA was to biology. Whether one views this claim as fact or a bit of hyperbole ultimately depends on your view of the potential power of empathy.

Either way, this important discovery was of mirror neurons, a revolutionary insight into the human brain—and into our understanding of others.

The Parma scientific team, soon known as "the Fab Four," included Vittorio Gallese, Giacomo Rizzolatti, Leonardo Fogassi, and Luciano Fadiga, and had for years been doing brain research on macaque monkeys. They picked up where primatologist Frans de Waal left off.

De Waal posited that what we recognize as altruistic behavior in primates is driven by their feeling what other primates feel. But is "feeling" really going on in the primate's brain, and is it more significant than their trained punishment-reward calculations?

Ultimately the only way to find out whether an empathic response was in fact a different and separate response from a learned response was to observe the activity in the brain at the time of a subject's altruistic action. While a monkey's brain is only one-fourth the size of a human brain, its structure and activity are quite similar. The interest of the Parma team was in understanding the brain activity associated with higher-level decisions, so they focused on the neocortex, which is found only in mammals and is the most recently evolved brain structure.

Using a harmless hair-thin electrode inserted into the monkey's brain and connected to an oscilloscope and speaker, the Fab Four tracked their subjects' brain activity. If there was a special process in the brain for empathy, it would most likely be found in the neocortex labeled F5.

They had been monitoring which parts of the brain fired when the monkeys took different actions, such as reaching for or grasping a food treat. They discovered that it was the F5 region of the macaque monkey's brain that fired regularly when the macaque reached for a treat, in this case raisins.

As legend has it, their initial discovery came as a complete surprise. One day when the team leader, Vittorio, was reaching for some raisins himself, suddenly the speakers sounded, alerting the researchers that the F5 region of the macaque's brain—within the premotor cortex—was firing exactly as it did when the monkey was himself reaching for raisins.

Could the same brain cells that fire when instructing the arm to take action to reach for the raisins also be activated at the perception of someone else reaching for that treat? Could the monkey's brain be constructing a form of simulation of the action it observed, imagining itself reaching for the treat? The answer to both questions proved to be yes.

The macaque saw Vittorio reaching for the raisins, and his brain created a perfect simulation of the action. The same part of the macaque's brain, F5, that had reacted when he was reaching for raisins himself also fired when he saw Vittorio taking the same action.[6]

Prior to this moment, the incumbent assumption was that perception—seeing and hearing the world around us, such as when

---

6   Marco Iacoboni, *Mirroring People: The New Science of How We Connect with Others* (New York: Farrar, Straus & Giroux, 2008).

recognizing your spouse—was located in the back of the brain, the temporal visual cortex. Action, on the other hand, involved sending the visual image to the front of the brain, the premotor cortex, where the brain initiates action on the image—giving your spouse a kiss. The third theorized component was cognition, located somewhere between perception and action, which permits us to plan, prioritize, or refine our action, for example choosing a romantic kiss on the lips rather than a little peck on the cheek.

In the past, the scientific community had assumed that all these functions were separate and independent from each other, consistent with popular theories about brain specialization.

However, this "accidental" finding in Parma suggested that the brain is much more facile, able to combine perception and action within the same neurons, all part of a single, elegant response. These neurons were actually mirroring the actions of others. Our brains appear to be able to create a simulation of another person's action, simulating emotions as if they were our own—feeling what the other person feels.

While the Parma team recognized over two decades ago that they had discovered something of enormous potential significance, they were not yet sure of its full implications. What special role do these mirror neurons play, and why have they developed in humans and some mammals?

The hunt was on. The next step was to duplicate these findings in humans.

A few years later Christian Keysers, who led the Netherlands Institute for Neuroscience lab, and Bruno Wicker of the Institut de Neurosciences de la Timone were discussing how they could take the learnings from the macaque monkey studies in Parma and test the idea of the existence of mirror neurons in humans. With the recent development of functional magnetic resonance imaging (fMRI), they realized that they could now look noninvasively inside the human brain. Keysers and Wicker designed an experiment to see if this same process of simulating emotions found in macaque brains existed in humans.

They were on the trail of empathy, what it is, and how it works. Keyser and Wicker described their plans for how they might make the leap between testing for empathy in monkeys and doing so in humans: "What we would need......is an experiment in which we place a participant in the scanner, evoke an emotion to measure the brain areas involved in experiencing emotion, and also show the same participant the emotions of others to discover if seeing the emotion activates the parts of the circuit involved in experiencing the emotion."[7]

So, obtaining the use of an MRI machine in Marseille, France, Keysers and Wicker enlisted twelve human volunteers.

The first step was to have volunteers placed in MRI scanners, where they would watch movies of actors sniffing the contents of a glass—some actors reacting with a pleasant expression, others with expressions of disgust—and then measure their brain activity. The next step was spraying into the volunteers' surgical masks mists with an array of smells, again from pleasant to disgusting, while monitoring their brains' reactions to those smells. With this approach they could measure both the subjects' observed emotions of others and their own emotions when experiencing the smells themselves.

The objective was to determine if the brain's reaction to the pungent smells in the mists was the same process as when the subjects reacted to seeing others experiencing the smells. In short, did the brain in fact mirror the experiences of others?

Again, the answer was yes. When the volunteers smelled the different scents, their anterior insula lit up, corresponding to their brain's reactions to the facial expressions of the actors they had observed. The volunteers' brains responded the same way to *observing* the reactions of others to specific odors as they did to *experiencing* the smells themselves. Not surprisingly, the most disgusting smells and most disgusted facial expressions evoked the strongest reactions by the mirror neurons. The more powerful the observed human reaction, the stronger the mirrored reaction.

---

7   Christian Keysers, *The Empathic Brain: How the Discovery of Mirror Neurons Changes Our Understanding of Human Nature* (Social Brain Press, 2011), 95.

Keysers and Wicker concluded that the process within the human brain was the same as in macaque monkeys—similar special neurons were "mirroring" the emotional response that the volunteers saw on the faces of others.

Other neuroscientists were making similar use of MRIs to identify those mirror neurons and study how they responded to seeing emotions in other humans. Neuroscientist Marco Iacoboni built even further on the macaque breakthrough. Also by using MRIs and human volunteers, he proved that the reactions of these mirror neurons in the premotor cortex are not just in response to grasping for food or observing the grasping for food, but also that they contained learned memories about the implied *intent* of the action.

Iacoboni's experiments included the context of an action. He set up two classic grasping scenes using videos, one with no context, just an arm reaching out about to grasp some unseen object. Then he tested the same action within the context of a small table neatly set for tea and another within the context of the same table, this time set as if the tea was finished, defined by a messy table with crumbs and a dirty napkin. (Of course, the test subjects had to be familiar with the meaning of a set table and one on which food had already been consumed.)

The results were as he expected: there was greater response in the mirror neurons for the grasping of the teacups in the two context settings than in the neutral grasping scene, and greater still in the one context scene with the neat table versus the messy table. The volunteers' brains assumed that the hand reaching toward the undisturbed table was more likely to be pouring tea than the hand reaching toward the messy table, which was assumed to be more likely cleaning up.

Iacoboni proved that mirror neurons can code intention into the actions that they witness rather than just respond similarly to the same familiar action. He may have identified the origin of that mysterious human instinct—intuition. Vittorio explained the connection in a lecture observed by Keysers: "Mirror neurons in your premotor cortex, in this very pragmatic area, appear to give us an intuitive understanding of the actions of other people."[8]

Empathy is clearly more useful if it permits us to feel the likely suffering of the other person before it occurs and so motivates our action to prevent it. On the one hand, we take for granted this capacity to imagine the future suffering of others, but when you place that gift within the context of possibly preventing that suffering, these seem more like the powers of a modern-day superhero.

This anticipation of future events is the bread and butter of suspense movie thrillers. Our stomach churns as we watch the villain in the movie point a gun at the innocent character because our brains are anticipating the fate of the likely victim. Mirror neurons are firing throughout the theater. Alfred Hitchcock, perhaps the greatest master of movie suspense, is known to have said: "There is no terror in a bang, only in the anticipation of it."[9] Hitchcock understood intuitively the strong and anticipatory impact mirror neurons can have on our emotions, even if the science had not yet discovered the process that makes it happen.

The evidence has been building that, in addition to humans, at least some other mammals have a very efficient and nearly instantaneous connection between what the eye sees or the ear hears and the brain's processing of that information—its passage from the primary visual cortex to the primary motor cortex. Now we know that connection can be made by just anticipating what might be about to happen.

Within the premotor cortex lie the mirror neurons that capture the image of the blood-streaked face of the child in the rubble of her bombed Syrian home and what you anticipate would happen to her if the child were not rescued. Your brain creates a simulation of what you see happening and anticipate will happen, placing you in the child's shoes, feeling her pain—feeling empathy for her plight.

Scientists are beginning to understand what philosophers already knew: people who demonstrate acts of humanity are somehow

8   Keysers, *Empathic Brain*, 19.
9   Elizabeth Knowles, ed., *Oxford Dictionary of Modern Quotations* (Oxford: Oxford University Press, 2007), 154.

connected in a special way with their empathy—a connection upon which humanity rests.

Increasingly, we are learning that staying connected with others of our species is critical to healthy communities and healthy individuals. Empathy may hold an important key to how we get connected and stay connected with people—even those beyond our tribe.

But this science still leaves some important unanswered questions. What is the purpose of this highly sophisticated, finely tuned human trait? Why is it blocked in some people and not in others? Lastly, how might we better connect with our empathy and with our fellow human beings?

The urgency of these questions about empathy are underscored by the insights of John Howard Griffin sixty years ago and the daily headlines of today. Escalating tribal conflict requires an equal and opposite force to stop its momentum. Could that force be empathy?

Chapter Five

Sit with Us

Life isn't just about taking in oxygen and giving out carbon dioxide.
—Malala Yousafzai[1]

There may be no people anywhere on planet Earth who are more tribal than American teenagers. We tend to think about tribalism in the context of racial, ethnic, or religious subgroups like the Tutsis and Hutus of Rwanda or the Sunni and Shia of Islam, but if tribalism is about extreme loyalty to one's own group to the exclusion of others, teenagers fit right in (irony intended).

Teenage cliques provide us with a familiar context for understanding worrisome tribal behavior and its challenge to empathic understanding of those "different from us." Most of us growing up in the United States have experienced, or at least witnessed, how the insecurity of teenagers and their concomitant desire to be accepted have manifested as hurtful insensitivity at their most tame, and cruelty, even bullying, at their worst. Teenage gangs, with their identity tattoos and brutal initiation rites, are an extreme example. More common are the everyday teasing and exclusion of others from group activity. Taken together, teenage cliques or gangs have led many parents, teachers, and law enforcement agents to throw up their hands and ask in exasperation, What can be done?

Well, a teenager from Sherman Oaks, California, decided to do something about it. Attending a private, all-girls middle school where, as she described it, she was "ostracized by pretty much everyone,"

---

1 Malala Yousafzai, *I Am Malala: How One Girl Stood Up for Education and Changed the World* (New York: Little, Brown, 2013), chap. 9.

Natalie Hampton did not fight back or tell off her tormentors; she created a smart phone app.[2]

In interviews, Natalie recounts vividly her story of being ostracized from the other girls in her school, treated like a pariah, and taunted. But for her, and no doubt for many thousands of other teenagers, one of the most painful experiences was being forced to sit alone in the cafeteria at lunchtime. While the other kids were laughing and enjoying one another, Natalie sat apart, trying to pretend everything was normal. But it was not.

It might seem a stretch to compare teenage cliques with tribes of white supremacists or angry anti-immigrant protesters, but not when we look more closely. Like these more extreme tribes, teenage cliques are driven by fear (of not fitting in) to band together with the like-minded (conformity), and too often, they act shockingly cruel in how they exclude others to reinforce their place in their tribe. Excluding others out of fear of being excluded is classic tribal behavior.

Interestingly, this cruelty often shocks even the perpetrator, as if the motivation came from some unknown place, deep down, hidden from their consciousness. It did, as we'll see.

For most teenagers, acceptance and connection with friends is often their highest priority. But why would they feel so intensely about the need to exclude potential friends? The answer is key to understanding today's adult ethnic, racial, and political tribes.

For decades, many experts in behavioral psychology and medical science have argued that connection and relationships between human beings is central to living a long and fulfilled life. Columnist and author Thomas Friedman recounts a story of asking the US surgeon general at the time, Dr. Vivek Murthy, what disease is the major cause of early death—heart disease, cancer, diabetes? Surprisingly, the surgeon general's answer was "none of the above." Rather, he explained, it is social isolation that most shortens our lives.[3]

2   "'Sit With Us' Creator Natalie Hampton's Crusade to Help Bullied Teens Feel Included," Knowledge@Wharton High School, September 27, 2016, http://kwhs.wharton.upenn.edu/2016/09/sit-us-creator-natalie-hamptons-crusade-help-bullied-teens-feel-included/.
3   Thomas Friedman, *Thank You for Being Late: An Optimist's Guide to Thriving in the Age of Accelerations* (New York: Farrar, Straus & Giroux, 2016).

Connection with others is essential not only to our longevity but also to our general physical wellness. We know that healthy relationships with family and friends are central to strong self-esteem and psychological health. The need for companionship and connection is another essential mammalian trait. No wonder Natalie and millions of other kids around the world find social estrangement so painful.

Natalie transferred schools, and things improved for her. She removed herself from that unhealthy environment, but she would never forget how it felt to be spurned by the members of a well-established social tribe to which she aspired. So in her new school, whenever she saw a fellow student sitting alone, her heart would hurt as she imagined the pain that student was feeling.

Ironically and hopefully, the act of tribal exclusion can also activate the empathy of those doing the exclusion: *I know how that feels.*

This pain gave birth to Sit With Us, an app that allows kids to invite others who are sitting alone to join their group or for them to discreetly ask to be invited—all on their smartphones. Further, the app encourages students to act as ambassadors who work for inclusion by connecting kids and discouraging exclusion.

Natalie understood that most teenagers who find themselves on the outside of their peer group cannot change schools, and few schools have the wisdom or resources to solve the larger problem of hurtful cliques. So Natalie decided to address the core of the problem: teenagers new to the school or who are different from the dominant group and are "othered" by the tribe—spurned by the group out of jealousy, fear, or ignorance. The essential fuel of the tribe, "othering" nontribal members, confirms the status of their group, empowering the tribe.

Again, the word *tribe* seems somewhat harsh when applied to teenagers, but *Merriam-Webster* defines tribalism as "tribal consciousness and loyalty; especially exaltation of the tribe above other groups."[4]

Teenagers who have experienced the shunning of their peer group are not likely to view *tribe* as an unfair descriptor. On the app's website,

---

4   *Merriam-Webster*, s.v. "tribe (n.)," accessed July 2, 2020, https://www.merriam-webster.com /dictionary/tribe.

Natalie very simply describes her motivation for acting: "Sit With Us was born because I am committed to making sure that other kids don't suffer as I did."[5]

In a sense, we might say that Sit With Us is an empathy-driven app. Now when a teenager's heart goes out to a peer sitting alone, connecting discreetly with them and inviting them to join their group is just a few clicks away.

This act by the larger community to "other" someone is as old as (indeed, far older than) Nathaniel Hawthorne's story of the seventeenth-century protagonist Hester Prynne, who is forced to wear the letter *A* for adultery as she is cruelly ostracized by her Puritan neighbors in his classic novel *The Scarlet Letter*.[6]

The Puritans were savvy people, particularly when it came to designing painful punishment that employed community scorn to discourage recidivism. They understood that physical punishment was painful, but it had a finite end and the wounds would heal. But when you put someone in the stocks on the town green with a sign around their neck screaming "blasphemer," they become the target of public scorn from their family, neighbors, and fellow parishioners. Those scars heal much more slowly.

Ironically, or appropriately, for years *The Scarlet Letter* was required reading for most American high school students. But the leap to today is a big ask. Scarlet letters have been replaced by "dissing" someone on a vastly more powerful stage than the town center; today the town center is Facebook, Twitter, and Snapchat. The social pillorying of today can be far more personal and meaner and can reach hundreds, thousands, or more. Being ostracized from the tribe can mean the loss of friends, career, and reputation, and most tragically, even the taking of one's life.

Social media, for all its extraordinary advantages, has revived the tribal scorn of seventeenth-century New England on an industrial scale.

Despite the lessons from *The Scarlet Letter*, successfully addressing the causes of teenage exclusion and bullying is a challenge that

5   Natalie Hampton, "About Sit With Us, Inc. – A 501(c)(3) Organization," Sit With Us, accessed December 10, 2020, http://sitwithus.io./#!/About.

6   Nathaniel Hawthorne, *The Scarlet Letter: A Romance* (Boston: Ticknor and Fields, 1850).

has eluded school officials, law enforcement, and legislators. So Natalie reached for a more modern tool to provide the solution. With digital media, she could create a way for teenagers who feel empathy for classmates sitting outside the tribe to inconspicuously invite them to join their group—no confrontation, no embarrassment.

She creatively used the same social media that had fanned the flames of tribal exclusion to temporarily breach the tribal walls and bring the shunned in from the cold.

Sit With Us caught on in other high schools across the country. Perhaps most encouraging, many students have embraced the ambassador component of the app in which the user helps teenagers take proactive steps to encourage broader acceptance in their schools and replace tribal exclusion with empathic connectedness.

Perhaps it is because the insecurities of growing up are so familiar to most of us that high schools make wonderful social behavior petri dishes. Under our empathic microscope, we see two sides to human nature in search of some form of connection: the creation of tribes of the like-minded seeking a sense of belonging, reaffirmation, and protection at the cost of excluding others, and students offering connection through empathy and acts of altruism for classmates experiencing that social shunning.

Also, most teenagers have yet to develop the adult sophistication to effectively hide their motivations, so they are particularly valuable study participants, often quickly surrendering the evidence that they are acting out long-standing evolutionary instincts, not just the feelings of the moment.

What is new is the growing evidence that there is a biological connection between teenage shunning and political, cultural, and religious extremism. Perhaps that is why teenagers are prime targets for terrorist recruitment.

If at the root, instinctive level there is a nexus between innocent American teenage behavior and that of ideological or religious extremists, those shared roots could hold the clues to how we might bridge those destructive divides.

We recoil at the hatred spewed by extremists, whether the ultraright or the extreme left, and wonder, How could they possibly harbor those absolutist beliefs and employ those violent tactics about the innocent targets of their rage? They must be delusional! The answer is that quite often they do not hold those beliefs, or at least those beliefs are not as simple as some claim.

Race, culture, and ethnicity are often the targets of extremist scorn, so it is only natural that we might conclude that what motivates their anger is simply bias against those specific groups. Our argument to extremists is often very cerebral, that the targets of their bias are off-limits, shielded by the equal protection clause of the US Constitution. Of course, while that might be true, to the extremists that can sound like a non sequitur. *I'm not interested in their rights; I just want them out of my world.*

But when we look more closely, we don't find a quibble over legal protection but a deep-seated, more generalized fear of difference—difference that often manifests as a challenge to long-held social status, traditions, or beloved identity myths of the past. These are the more fundamental, even primordial, drivers of their hatred.

However complicated their motivations, tribal members often explain their reactions in oversimplified slogans that reflect only the symptoms of what they fear, not the real causes: *Protect American jobs. Defend our religion from apostates. Punish the corrupt Tutsis. She just doesn't fit in.* These rationalizations provide a patina of justification for people to act on their more amorphous fear of others or loss of social status. They provide permission to the speaker to give voice to their most extreme feelings, without touching on the real cause that brings them to the rally or demonstration.

They claim a position of strength but are reacting out of a sense of weakness. They create convenient strawmen for their rage because, like the soldier with posttraumatic stress disorder or the NFL football player with chronic traumatic encephalopathy, they do not fully understand the roots of their emotions. They come from too far down.

Of course, some people whom we conveniently call extremists suffer from psychological illness, which, in those cases, explains their actions. However, mental illness certainly does not explain the tens of thousands of people who scream frightening epithets at political rallies or the thousands radicalized by religious leaders of many faiths.

It seems that the people we know as generally kind and well-mannered neighbors and friends have, at least temporarily, de-coupled from their normal behavior and are acting in ways that are inconsistent with their personal moral code or religious beliefs—their better angels have been silenced.

It is when a raw nerve is struck—being racially profiled, losing their job because their plant was moved overseas, or being excluded from their teenage clique. In emotionally demanding situations like these, often our rational understanding of events and our empathy for the "other guy" is overridden, and our deep-seated fear and anger at being excluded or left behind rises to the surface. And when those ancient emotions are activated, conflict, even violence, is not far behind.

This type of outlier behavior, from the political extremist to the terrorist, is often driven by a disconnection from society and social norms, because they cannot find within their existing social resources the self-reaffirmation, reassurance, and self-confidence that they need to quiet their fears about a changing world.[7]

These isolated souls gravitate to tribes of people like them to find connection with those who might help them cope with those fears. We are witnessing the impact of rapidly accelerating social change clashing with much, much more slowly evolving evolutionary traits.

You can draw a direct biological line from the fear of a high school teenager being shown up by a new transfer student to his parents' fear of losing their jobs to new immigrants, and all the way to the Iraqi Shia family's fear of the Sunni official taking control of their town.

They are all fearful of what these "others" represent within a world of disconcerting change that is difficult for them to understand. This

---

7   Ryan Smith, article title to be determined, International Institute for Counter-Terrorism publication ICT, forthcoming, in the author's possession, https://www.ict.org.il /ContentWorld.aspx?ID=1#gsc.tab=0.

fear often begets suspicion, which begets anger, which, too often, leads to conflict.

Fortunately, fear of difference is not the only evolutionary trait wrestling for humanity's attention.

You can draw a similar but far more hopeful biological commonality between the white men and women who braved great physical violence to march alongside Blacks in Selma, Alabama; the volunteers who risk their lives around the world working for Doctors Without Borders; and Ricky Best and Taliesin Namkai-Meche, who gave their lives defending two young Muslim women who were being harassed by a deranged white supremacist in Portland, Oregon. They are humanity's heroes, and their sacrifices encourage the rest of us. They resisted the call of their primal fear, found empathy for "others," and translated that empathy into action.

In these instances, the evolutionary durability of empathy proved a clear advantage to humankind. We still have much more to learn about the interplay of our deep-seated fears and our empathy.

Neurologist and neuroscientist Marco Iacoboni put it simply and clearly: "Mirror neuron research...suggests that our social codes are largely dictated by our biology."[8] For good and bad.

If Natalie, and humanity's other heroes, can resist the tug of evolutionary fear, then we should try to understand how empathy operates and discover the details of its interplay with its antagonist, tribalism. What is the origin of empathy, how does it work, how early in a person's development does it present itself, how does empathy counter evolutionary fear, and can it be taught?

Jean Piaget, the Swiss developmental psychologist who for decades was considered by many to be the leading authority on when children develop the capacity for different emotions and cerebral activity, believed that sympathy (he conflated sympathy with empathy) in children did not emerge until the age of seven or eight, when they could see things from the other person's perspective. A reasonable hypothesis, but recent science suggests that empathy is more complex and dynamic.

---

8 Iacoboni, *Mirroring People*, chap. 11.

Today it seems that Piaget's view of empathy as a considered, cognitive response that does not present before the age of seven or eight was mistaken. New studies of young children, even babies, support the conclusion that empathy is more likely an instinctive, emotional response, hardwired from birth.

Many parents, as well as scientists, had assumed that when a newborn burst into tears in reaction to the crying of other babies in the nursery, it was from being startled by a loud noise. But recent studies in which newborns were exposed to computer-simulated baby cries and other loud noises did not evoke the same intensity of response as did the crying of real babies. A New York University psychologist, Martin Hoffman, told the *New York Times*, "Virtually from the day they are born, there is something particularly disturbing to infants about the sound of another infant's cry....The innate predisposition to cry to that sound seems to be the earliest precursor of empathy."[9]

This is not definitive evidence that the tearful newborns were having an empathic response to the distress of other babies, but it is consistent with studies in which toddlers respond to crying nursery mates by bringing their mates their favorite toys to cheer them up. In one study a toddler takes his mother to an anguished child to soothe, despite the presence of the distressed child's own mother right next to him.[10]

It can be difficult to parse the difference between empathy and acting to protect the aggrieved out of a sense of justice—a sense of morality, of right and wrong. But these two responses, empathic and fair-minded, are clearly related.

We have found some important evidence about the capacity of very young babies to differentiate between right and wrong in related studies at the Infant Cognition Center at Yale (a.k.a. the Baby Lab), which has done research into the related question of whether we are born with a sense of morality. The early evidence appears to suggest

9   Natalie Angier, "Empathy Unfolds Slowly in a Child," *New York Times*, May 9, 1995.
10 Daniel Goleman, "Researchers Trace Empathy's Roots to Infancy," *New York Times*, March 28, 1989.

that we are, as we see from research into the reaction of babies to scenarios in which puppets are used to demonstrate good and bad behavior.

In this experiment, babies only a few months old witness a puppet struggling to open a box. Another puppet, the "good" puppet, helps it open the box, while another, the "bad" puppet, slams the box shut. Afterward, lab staff who are intentionally unaware of which of the puppets are good and which bad, offer both the puppets separately to each of the babies that saw the show. More than 80 percent of the babies in that experiment selected the good puppet when given the chance to choose either one.

This research was conducted to test for the early development of morality, and the results suggest that these babies know the difference between good and bad and found good to be more desirable. In this case, the researchers assigned "good" to the puppets who were helpful and "bad" to the puppets who undermined the baby's desires.[11]

So apparently, young babies can differentiate between what the researchers constructed as good and bad behavior, and they prefer the helpful puppet over the puppet who made things more difficult. That provides interesting evidence that very young babies have some inherent sense of good and bad, but it begs another question: Were the babies' choices of the good puppet over the bad puppet driven by a sense of injustice and/or their empathy for the struggling baby?

It is intriguing to consider that this early morality reflected by the good puppet was driven by empathy for the puppet struggling to open the box. Could the babies feel the puppet's frustration in being thwarted in opening the box, putting themselves in the shoes of the struggling baby? Is this test of morality equally a test of empathy for the struggling puppet?

At least in this research, was empathy the driver of preferring good behavior?

---

11 Kelly Wallace, "What Your Baby Knows Might Freak You Out," CNN, February 14, 2014, http://www.cnn.com/2014/02/13/living/what-babies-know-anderson-cooper-parents/index .html.

While not a specific conclusion of Yale's Baby Lab, this study seems to suggest to us that empathy is an emotional catalyst for the early judgment of good and bad behavior. This research appears to show a fascinating connection between a mirrored emotional response to the puppet's frustration and a reasoned, cerebral conclusion that helping another is morally good.

This conclusion, that reducing another's pain equals morally good behavior, connects empathy with altruism, the action that the good puppet appeared to take in helping the puppet open the box.

Using my own personal experience as a child to illustrate the principle, one day at recess in my third grade class I saw the class bully, Peter, take the hat of a boy I knew whose family operated one of the last farms in our rapidly suburbanizing community. My neighbor Jimmy was a nice kid, even if a little different in dress and habits from most of the suburban kids. Peter had taken Jimmy's hat and was running around, taunting the boy. I still recall vividly how I had an immediate emotional empathic response for Jimmy and an almost simultaneously cognitive conclusion: *That could be me, and it's hurtful, not fair...I must stop it...but Peter is not going to like it.* In the world of a third grader, this happened in about ten seconds, followed by my tackling Peter, which precipitated a lot of rolling around on the ground and a trip to the principal's office.

As an interesting corollary to this story of empathy and altruism, while seated together outside the principal's office awaiting our punishment, Peter and I bonded against the common enemy, school authority—which resided outside of our tribe of elementary school boys.

That early childhood experience stayed with me for years, and only in writing this book did I understand how it appears to support the idea that the long-standing mammalian capacity to mirror the feelings of others is hardwired in the human brain and can trigger an altruistic response despite the possibility of an adverse outcome. This balance of the emotional and the reasoned is essential to the larger story of how we use empathy to make a better world.

Further, it illustrates the growing research in humans that posits that when an individual is aware of the suffering of another (even at a very early age), often feelings of empathy will trigger consideration of response alternatives.

This connection of empathy (feeling what others feel) to altruism (an action that seems morally right or just) is a central underpinning to humane societies and the rule of law. It represents the triumph of our better angels over our worst fears and instincts.

This brings us full circle to why so many of Natalie's peers at her first school, described as normal, caring kids, failed to respond to their empathic signals. Is it a taboo of the tribe that inhibits the teenagers' empathy, or does the student join the tribe because they share with the others some relevant characteristics—acute insecurity of their place in life and/or prejudice toward certain "others"—which are sufficient to block empathy?

In Natalie Hampton we saw all the elements of the empathy to altruism chain. She was made *aware* of "othering" from her own experience in her first school, her *empathy* was triggered by observing kids sitting alone at her new school, then her *perspective* led her to envision a solution, which motivated her *altruism*, which took the form of championing the cause of inclusion by creating a smartphone app.

While Natalie chose to make her app free, one might consider that she could have made money on the idea. So, it is reasonable to ask, Is creating an app that might prove to be financially rewarding really altruism? In my judgment, absolutely. The important element is the objective of the action. If in response to one's empathy the principal objective is to help another, it is altruism.

Taken in their totality, actions grounded in a desire to do "good" move humanity forward.

Chapter Six

Defusing Tribalism

Me and my clan against the world;
Me and my family against my clan;
Me and my brother against my family;
Me against my brother.
—Somali proverb

As I write this book, I find it impossible to ignore the deaths of two college fraternity pledges, the victims of overly zealous fraternity initiations. Sophomore Tim Piazza of Penn State and freshman Maxwell Gruver of Louisiana State University forfeited their lives before they really got started.

Some point a finger at excessive drinking, others at irresponsible fraternity members or fraternity hazing run amok. Certainly all were contributing factors, but why are some young college students so desperate to join a fraternity, and why are the fraternity members so insistent on extreme rituals and so callous toward their pledges? Is it because the pledges have yet to make the transition from outsider to insider?

We have learned from research on babies that humans are born with a sense of tribe—feelings of compatibility with those who are related or like us and concomitant feelings of suspicion, distrust, and even fear of those who are different.

This we know. But what explains the intensity of that need to be part of the tribe and to denigrate other tribes or the unaffiliated?

Evidence is growing that this suspicion of difference is an inherited trait, passed down over millennia, which has historically served the purpose of alerting early humans to the danger from other prehistoric tribes competing for food or territory.

Therefore, fear of difference appears to be a foundational trait of basic survival. That is about as intense as things get. But why did that intensity, so important to the survival of early humans, continue over thousands of generations to today, when we have police to protect us, grocery stores to nourish us, and schools to educate us on the "others" who share our world?

The problem with some evolutionary traits in humans is that they overstay their usefulness. The traditional evolutionary roles of men as warrior and hunter, and women as nurturer of the children, have given way to a modern mix of roles, as female marines and male nannies attest. Nevertheless, even in 2021 that transition has been uneven and disconcerting to many people and many cultures—from law enforcement to Hollywood.

While human reason has overtaken much of the primitive alarm system of suspicion and replaced it with more sophisticated methods for detecting threats (widely accepted codes of conduct and improved communications, for instance) and means of protection (the rule of law and modern policing methods), biology is a stubborn force.

Suspicion, fear, and even hatred of people different from us persist among humans in the twenty-first century. This suspicion often becomes tribal, biologically driven and culturally reinforced—*my people against your people*.

Tribal suspicion and overreaction still exist in our communities and in every nation around the world. In America, major cities and some small towns are divided between neighborhoods of different races and cultures, with many areas "no go" for people of different tribes. Murders between members of street gangs, which exist nearly everywhere in America, account for the majority of killings in major cities such as Chicago and Los Angeles.

In fact, despite a multidecade decline in violent crime in America, violence has begun to rise again with the major driver being once again gang violence, which contributes a disproportionate percentage

of the daily mass killings in America (killings with four or more victims). Tribal warfare is on the rise, in America and around the world.[1]

Similarly, as wars between nation-states appear to be waning, in-
trastate tribal conflict is growing. It is responsible for much of the
worst violence in modern times, including genocide between Tutsis
and Hutus in Rwanda, Christians and Muslims in Nigeria, Protestants
and Catholics in Northern Ireland, and Sikhs and Hindus in India.
It is ubiquitous.

Traditional tribalism means a connection between people that
often separates them from others, frequently based on racial, ethnic,
or cultural identity. Today we see increasing numbers of tribes that
are organized around a strong sense of a shared identity or beliefs:
moral values, social norms, political views, or mutual antagonisms.

Avid fans of the Denver Broncos could be called a tribe based
on their shared enthusiasm for their football team and concomitant
animosity for their team's competitors. A harmless tribalism, unless
of course you are wearing a New England Patriots jersey at a Denver
home game. Far less harmless are soccer matches in Europe that
are too often plagued by tribes of Russian football fans who come
prepared to do battle with opposing soccer tribes using weapons and
martial arts training.

This alarming trend of tribal antagonism in sports is developing
side by side with growing cosmopolitan diversity. Today we seem
increasingly at war with each other.

Despite the considerable variation among types of tribes, the
intensity of feelings that tribal affiliation can encourage presents a
growing challenge to a peaceful society, as people of different racial,
ethnic, cultural, religious, and political beliefs are thrown together
by twenty-first-century migration and global travel.

---

1   Lois Beckett, "Most Victims of US Mass Shootings Are Black, Data Analysis Finds," *Guardian*,
    May 23, 2016, https://www.theguardian.com/us-news/2016/may/23/mass-shootings-tracker
    -analysis-us-gun-control-reddit; "Hidden America: Don't Shoot, I Want to Grow Up,"
    information graphic, ABC News, accessed September 14, 2020, http://abcnews.go.com
    /Nightline/fullpage/chicago-gang-violence-numbers-17509042; "Measuring the Extent
    of Gang Problems," National Gang Center, accessed September 25, 2020, https://www
    .nationalgangcenter.gov/survey-analysis/measuring-the-extent-of-gang-problems.

How can you understand the other person if the other person represents a perceived threat to you, or if you view him or her as a composite of all the human characteristics that you dislike or disrespect? If empathy can serve as a pathway to understanding and cooperation, how can we keep open our channel to empathic feelings?

The journey from suspicion of difference to celebrating difference is a long and windy one at best.

My unlikely choice to serve as our guide to take us on that journey from tribal hatred to empathic understanding is a dirt poor, white segregationist, and former exalted cyclops in the Ku Klux Klan from Durham, North Carolina: Claiborne Paul Ellis—known as C. P. Ellis to both friends and detractors.

Ellis's father worked in a textile mill in Durham during the early twentieth century and died at the age of forty-eight, most likely from what became known in later years as brown lung disease. Every day at work, Ellis's father inhaled vast amounts of cotton dust, an environmental hazard of a job that provided his family with only a very meager living. He worked hard but never had much money, not even enough to buy adequate clothing for himself or his kids.

Ellis was born in 1927, and his early childhood was shaped by the deprivation of the Great Depression, when his family slid from poor to "dirt poor." The Depression stole not only money for basics like clothing and adequate food, but it stole much of their dignity and self-respect as well.[2]

Ellis described his growing up dirt poor in the Deep South in an interview with Studs Terkel.

When I went to school, I never seemed to have adequate clothes to wear. I always left school late afternoon with a sense of inferiority. The other kids had nice clothes, and I just had what Daddy could buy. I still got some of those inferiority feelin's now that I have to overcome once in a while.

---

2   Studs Terkel, "C. P. Ellis, 'Why I Quit the Klan,'" in *American Dreams: Lost and Found* (New York: New Press, 1980).

> I loved my father. He would go with me to ball games. We'd go fishin' together. I was really ashamed of the way he'd dress. I always had the feeling about somebody looking at him and makin' fun of him and makin' fun of me. I think it had to do somethin' with my life.[3]

These are difficult feelings for a young child to experience, and they began to shape Ellis's early perception of what he considered to be his tribe: very poor southerners, which soon morphed into very poor white people.

> I really began to get bitter. I didn't know who to blame. I tried to find somebody. I began to blame it on Black people. I had to hate somebody. Hatin' America is hard to do because you can't see it to hate it. You gotta have somethin' to look at to hate. [He laughed.] The natural person for me to hate would be Black people, because my father before me was a member of the Klan. As far as he was concerned, it was the savior of the white people. It was the only organization in the world that would take care of the white people. So, I began to admire the Klan....
>
> The first night I went with the fellas, they knocked on the door and gave the signal. They sent some robed Klansmen to talk to me and give me some instructions. I was led into a large meeting room, and this was the time of my life! It was thrilling....
>
> I can understand why people join extreme right-wing or left-wing groups. They're in the same boat I was. Shut out. Deep down inside, we want to be part of this great society. Nobody listens, so we join these groups.[4]

Ellis's tribe of the have-nots only began to take real form and gather strength when it had a narrative that explained "why" they were unjustly

---

3   Terkel, "C. P. Ellis, 'Why I Quit the Klan,'" 198.
4   Terkel, "C. P. Ellis, 'Why I Quit the Klan,'" 201.

poor; and, as with most such extremist tribes, the "why" was provided by identifying an enemy, the cause of their lack of self-respect.

Ellis's comment "Deep down inside, we want to be part of this great society. Nobody listens, so we join these groups" is very telling. Ellis, a member of an extremist tribe (a hate group), says explicitly that he was driven into the arms of the KKK because he could not be part of the society at large. He felt disconnected and went looking for some connection with like-minded folks, which held the promise of recovering his self-respect and providing some explanation for the "rapid" changes he saw around him—particularly racial integration.

People often ask, Why didn't the poor whites fight the system that was responsible for their condition rather than Blacks who suffered as well? Of course, some did, but the challenge of fighting the system was daunting, and the pull of "any place but last place" was immediate and irresistible. If you think of it in evolutionary terms, the lions and tribal enemies would likely pick off the straggler; best not be last.

But Ellis, who died in 2005, was anything but a one-dimensional person. He was alarmed by what he saw and became ashamed of what he did. He was aware of the complexity of the growing racial divisiveness around him while he struggled with some latent empathy for Blacks who also had to travel a very hard road.

Awareness and empathy were two inconvenient qualities in an exalted cyclops of the KKK in the South, particularly during the turbulent 1950s and '60s. He explained to Terkel:

> I still didn't like blacks. I didn't want to associate with 'em. Blacks, Jews, or Catholics. My father said: "Don't have anything to do with 'em." I didn't until I met a Black person and talked with him, eyeball to eyeball, and met a Jewish person and talked to him, eyeball to eyeball. I found out they're people just like me. They cried, they cussed, they prayed, they had desires. Just like myself....But at that time, my mind was closed.[5]

---

5   Terkel, "C. P. Ellis, 'Why I Quit the Klan,'" 204.

In 1971, with the tension and violence that surrounded court-ordered busing to desegregate public schools cresting, the city council of Durham, North Carolina, decided to hold public meetings during which citizens could speak their minds on this incendiary issue. The KKK was there in force on one side of the room, while Black community activists, tempered by earlier civil rights campaigns, filled the seats on the other side of the auditorium. There was much name-calling, threats, and accusations and very little mutual understanding.

That is when providence intervened in the form of one brilliant and exceptionally intuitive community organizer, Bill Riddick. Armed with a $78,000 grant from the federal government to aid desegregation, he proposed a series of community discussion groups in the hopes of finding a peaceful solution.

Given the political climate, discussion groups didn't appear to represent much of a solution. But Riddick must have understood that familiarity tends to dissolve tribal barriers, as Ellis later learned: "I found out they're people just like me."[6] Riddick kept after it.

He also understood that if you mix up the tribes and create ad hoc groups with shared interests, it weakens the clarity of distance and replaces it with a more nuanced, human intimacy of proximity.

Riddick's brilliance became evident in his stunning suggestion that the group discussions be cochaired by two very unlikely peacemakers: Ann Atwater, an outspoken, hardened Black civil rights activist, and KKK cyclops C. P. Ellis. To the further surprise of most in attendance, after considerable soul-searching and uncertainty, they both accepted.

Still, bridging tribal walls is rarely a simple matter. Despite being well-regarded leaders of their respective tribes, Ellis and Atwater were immediately showered with harsh criticism and name-calling from both opponents and supporters. Reaching out to the other tribe was suspect; suspicion ran deep. No one knew what would happen next, but they feared the worst because "the worst" always seemed to follow.

---

6   Terkel, "C. P. Ellis, 'Why I Quit the Klan,'" 204.

Ellis didn't trust or respect Atwater, and she had only contempt for him. Riddick had created the opportunity, but someone had to step across the tribal lines first. Eventually, Ellis took those fitful and fateful first steps.

He called Atwater, acknowledged their differences, but reminded her that they had been presented with an opportunity that could benefit all their children and it was up to the two of them to make it happen. To Ellis's surprise, Atwater replied, "I'm willing if you are," and he sealed the deal with, "Let's do it."[7]

Their accommodation did not come without a steep personal price for both Ellis and Atwater. For the former Klan leader, the reward for his willingness to work with Atwater was an outpouring of disbelief and outrage. He noted, "My old friends would call me at night: 'C. P., what the hell is wrong with you? You're sellin' out the white race.'"[8]

Atwater paid a price too. She would describe how her daughter came home crying from school every day after her mom had joined forces with Ellis. Her daughter's teacher would make fun of her in front of the all–Black classroom because Atwater had found common cause with a former Klansman.

It was at that point, after Atwater conveyed her heartfelt story of her daughter's pain, that Ellis put together the critical pieces missed by so many other poor whites who had turned to white supremacy as a means to resolve their feelings of being left behind: "I begin to see, here we are, two people from far ends of the fence, havin' identical problems, except her bein' black and me bein' white. From that moment on, I tell ya, that gal and I worked together good. I begin to love the girl, really. [He wept.]"[9] With only an eighth-grade education and all the hardship and indignities of a childhood of grinding poverty, Ellis found his empathy for the hardships and indignities that Atwater had experienced over a lifetime at the hands of white segregationists. Remarkably, Ellis's candor made possible Atwater's empathy for this man who represented so much pain for Blacks throughout the South.

---

7   Terkel, "C. P. Ellis, 'Why I Quit the Klan,'" 206.
8   Terkel, "C. P. Ellis, 'Why I Quit the Klan,'" 207.
9   Terkel, "C. P. Ellis, 'Why I Quit the Klan,'" 208.

Between them they found a path toward understanding and co-operation. Their achievement seems even more remarkable when we each think of the many times that we found it "impossible" to be understanding of a family member or acquaintance whose views we considered offensive. In this case it might have been Ellis believing that Blacks received special government treatment, or Atwater's view that whites were responsible for every misfortune Blacks experienced. Being unable or unwilling to empathize with another's point of view, we often withdraw to the sanctuary of the like-minded: "Honey, can you believe that our neighbor believes such ridiculous ideas?"

Even our seemingly mild experiences in which we recoil in the face of repugnant ideas represent a challenge to empathy like that which Ellis and Atwater faced. Given the speed of communications and social interactions today, that recoil is often an instant reflex, creating a protective barrier to an alien idea or an unfair snap judgment about the speaker. In reacting so, we are walling others out and ourselves in.

No other issue in America's history has been more divisive than race. It is our nation's "third rail"—pulsing with high-voltage senti-ment. It is the source of our most tragic tribal conflict. It powered the catastrophes of slavery and the Civil War, plus thousands of conflicts over skin color to follow, including lynching, race riots, Jim Crow, the Black Panthers, white supremacists, and the struggle that ensued in reaction to the Black Lives Matter movement. As Ellis learned, it doesn't matter which side you are on of any divisive issue; it causes pain to everyone—and hobbles the progress of humankind.

To this day, race is the issue that most drives Americans back into their safe tribal cocoons—on both sides of the issue. Given the historic depth of fear and old animosities, it is even more extraordinary that KKK leader C. P. Ellis and civil rights activist Ann Atwater still found within themselves the empathy to look past their tribal feelings, and a great deal of American history, to find common cause.

For Ellis, the bridge from suspicion and hostility to cooperation reflected two remarkable empathic qualities. The first was his deliber-ate awareness, a willingness to see the contradictions in his prejudicial views toward Atwater and the needless pain caused by this tribal conflict. This gave Ellis the capacity to break through his inherited willful blindness, shared by so many poor white southerners, and see the burden borne by both Blacks and whites in the segregated South—particularly the burden carried by their children.

The second empathic quality, understanding, was reflected in both his insight into his father's poverty-driven despair and bigotry and the pain that Atwater was feeling as the victim of both poverty and bigotry. Growing increasingly aware of the truth about the world around him, Ellis would draw on the power of that empathy to give him the courage to act.

I recount Ellis's story at greater length than Atwater's simply because the distance he traveled from angry tribal leader to integration advocate was so unexpected. However, the steps that Atwater took, despite the understandable suspicions she had of Ellis and other white supremacists, hundreds of years in the making, was no less extraordinary. These two remarkable human beings demonstrated that even in the race-charged South, and on the explosive issue of school integration, they could reach across to someone in the other tribe and learn to trust them. They hold hope for the rest of us.

The first societal step in understanding how to seize that hope for the future is deliberate awareness of America today and its past—to understand the suffering our tribal alliances have caused and why we are again becoming more divisive and more tribal.

Only after we understand our tribal history and the deep-seated fears that drove it, and continue to drive it today, can we step across the yawning divide in this country.

If race in America is the third rail, the Vietnam War of the 1960s and '70s is an historic event that rode that third rail and divided America along other lines as well. This was another time of growing divisions in our nation, curiously right on the heels of the common sacrifice of World War II and the Great Depression—events that united us. But by the 1960s that solidarity, that purpose and common sacrifice, began to show signs of strain as many asked, Where to from here?

The Vietnam War sowed confusion and fear in the hearts of millions of draft-age young men threatened with the possibility that they would be sent to fight and die in the jungle for a cause they didn't understand or felt was misguided, even immoral. Others took a very different view, fearing that the demonstrations against the war and the stalemate on the battlefield were a harbinger of a decline in some of America's fundamental moral values—loyalty, service, and the commitment to win.

The big question during that divisive time was the same as the question we hear so often today: What is happening to America?

In the 1960s it soon became clear that those divisions around Vietnam and the stubborn issue of race had reached tribal proportions. The reconciliation that C. P. Ellis and Ann Atwater achieved on the issue of school busing in Durham, North Carolina, was all too rare. Those divisions haven't gone away.

The intense tribal conflict we see today on race, immigration, health care, and economic equality should be of no surprise to any of us. The proximate seeds of today's tribal conflict had been sown decades ago. By now, the tribal lines have been vividly drawn, absolutist positions reinforced by extremist media personalities, and unimaginably derogatory language aimed at our opponents, with no hint of compromise.

Today that tribal conflict is being animated not only by unresolved vestigial issues around race and America's role in the world but also by a powerful combination of new worldwide forces that seem to push nearly every evolutionary hot button: global migration, economic inequality, and technological disruption.

By the 1970s, most of Europe and Asia had rebuilt from the destruction of World War II, economic development was spreading throughout the world, and colonial empires were in full retreat. By the dawn of the new millennium, consumer prices were being driven down by new technology and lower-wage manufacturers around the world, people were traveling farther from home, educational levels were rising, economic refugees were on the move, and incomes were rising in most of the world.

Yet, as with all seismic social and economic change, this postwar world produced both winners and losers.

The tribal conflicts of today seem to be the culmination of those post–World War II changes: jobs are being eliminated and others created by lower-wage competition and new technology; social media is transforming how people connect with one another; new service and internet-based economies are creating both enormous wealth and economic inequality; the horror of terrorism continues to metastasize; and most disconcerting for many, the face of our communities is changing, becoming more diverse, less "like us."

In nearly every region of our country, manufacturing plants have gone quiet, generations of employees laid off, schools closed, and stores shuttered. Many cities and towns continue long slides into decline. Adding to that disruption, the Great Recession of 2007–2009 slammed the door on the promise of comfortable retirements for many baby boomers and reduced the prospects for their children as well.

All of this happened while many other Americans, often concentrated in larger cities and new suburbs, were getting wealthier. Centers of education, technology, and new industries in places such as Silicon Valley, Boston, and New York were born and inevitably evolved into centers of new wealth and globalization.

It was true that American prosperity was continuing but unevenly distributed to a smaller and smaller segment of the population. The centers of technology and global commerce tended to be clustered, also not equally distributed. This created a class of "left behinds" in America, Europe, and other developed nations, people who had ample reason to feel that the ground was moving out from under them. Day-to-day life was becoming very different from the world in which they grew up. Something seemed very wrong…and unjust.

In 2017, white nationalists protesting these social and economic changes marched in Charlottesville, Virginia, to a very telling refrain: "You will not replace us."[10] The media, many elected leaders, and opponents focused on the language used by these groups to define

---

10 "You Will Not Replace Us," Anti-Defamation League, accessed March 17, 2021, https://www.adl.org/education/references/hate-symbols/you-will-not-replace-us.

them principally as "haters." But while many used the language of hate and racial supremacy, a closer look at their slogan reveals a deeper understanding: the fear of being excluded.

Frightened of losing their place in American society and the respect and recognition that comes with successfully earning a living and raising a family. Frightened by the prospect that American opportunity was being denied to a previously revered segment of the nation: white, Christian, high school educated—the predominant profile of the post–World War II middle-class American worker.

We've seen this all before in the southern segregationists chronicled by John Howard Griffin and lived by C. J. Ellis—fear of losing one's standing in the community and in the economy.

Only an exceptionally empathic society can be expected to understand the real causes of this type of systemic tribal hatred and resolve them. Yet while these economic and social changes were unfolding, there were simultaneous cultural and media changes that cut against the organic development of our national empathy.

In addition to the very tangible disruption of work and community, a parallel trend was emerging that was more subtle but no less impactful on people's anxieties about what the future might bring. Whether in small towns, suburbia, or large cities, much of the connective tissue of our communities—church, local civic clubs, neighborhood get-togethers, and sports leagues—began to decline as cable TV, the internet, and more individual pastimes began to fill their spots.

Harvard political science professor Robert D. Putnam wrote a celebrated book in 2000, *Bowling Alone*, in which he used the bowling league as an analogy to suggest that since the 1960s these centers of connection in communities were collapsing, reducing what he called the "social capital" essential to people and their communities.[11]

These centers of connection in communities across the country are places to which one proudly belongs, by which one feels supported,

---

11   Robert D. Putnam, *Bowling Alone: The Collapse and Revival of American Community* (New York: Simon & Schuster, 2000).

and through which one develops a sense of meaning that satisfies a healthy evolutionary need to be part of a tribe with a purpose.

While a decade later Putnam wrote that he thought there was some evidence that this trend had begun to reverse, it appears that much damage has already been done to the glue that keeps individuals anchored to a sense of connectedness and well-being. Further, while Americans may be reconnecting with others, that reconnection appears to be more intensely tribal than a few decades ago. Often their involvement is around political partisanship designed primarily to serve individual interests in opposition to some other group rather than service with a civic group to help the larger community.

Of course, many of those traditional civic groups were made up of like-minded individuals of similar racial and cultural backgrounds. But the loss of those centers of connection, whose clearly understood mission was serving the community, left a void. That void appears to be at least partially filled by more tribal organizations whose central purpose is resisting change to convention or traditional ways of doing things. Too often those groups are overt about the exclusion of "others"—building walls to shut others out and themselves securely in.

For many Americans and others in developed countries, a sense of community has been at least partially replaced by a sense of a more impersonal, less connected, big society—where each of us is on his or her own to succeed or fail, with a diffused sense of purpose beyond individual success. Internet chat rooms, Twitter followers, talk radio fans, and Facebook communities have subtlety redefined the notion of human connectedness. It is more individual based, from a distance, and it allows more artifice than in-person common purpose. For many, this is community in name only, which over time further accentuates a feeling of isolation that can breed anxiety and despair.

Social scientists have found growing evidence among soldiers returning from Iraq and Afghanistan that the experience of losing an extremely tight social bond and high purpose—staying alive and protecting their buddies—and abruptly returning to civilian life where community bonds are fraying and a sense of the purpose less clear plays a substantial role in the development of posttraumatic stress disorder.

This desire to reconnect with that intense bond of mutual survival leads some soldiers to sign up for repeated combat tours in search of the common purpose and community support that they find missing in civilian life. To some degree, that phenomenon has existed during all wars; but with less "social capital" to support their transition home, today's veterans are more on their own. This is fertile ground for the germination of tribes, good and bad.

The attack on the nation's Capitol on January 6, 2021, frighteningly reflected all of this: sporting badges of tribal affiliation, Oath Keepers, Proud Boys, QAnon, and MAGA supporters declared years of grievances and harbored fantastical thinking about a stolen election that they felt justified their illegal behavior. Many media observers confessed surprise at the high number of ex-military and even some law enforcement breaching the Capitol walls, when these are the very segments of American society struggling the most with this seismic social change.

This economic and social dislocation sets off evolutionary bells for many, conveying the sense that they are exposed, at risk, in danger, or under attack. This seems a useful insight into the rise of private militias in America—relatively small groups of armed men and women who train to combat what they see as dangerous government "overreach" and other perceived threats. Members of militias often feel isolated and alienated from the changing world around them and, like C. P. Ellis, they need something or someone outside their tribe whom they can designate as the source of the threat.

In January of 2016, one militia led an armed takeover of the Malheur National Wildlife Refuge in Oregon. Among them were two sons of Cliven Bundy, a rancher who earlier had led an armed standoff with federal marshals who took exception to his refusing to pay the legally required fee to graze his cattle on federal lands—fees he had failed to pay for two decades.

In the Oregon standoff, one militia member refused to be taken alive and died in a shootout after weeks of negotiations. There are many more radical tribes in this country including the National Alliance, the World Church of the Creator, and the Aryan Nations on the right and the Animal Liberation Front and Earth Liberation Front on the left.

Why have so many traditional centers of connection like churches and civic clubs been replaced or supplemented by tribes organized around fear, hatred, and the threat of violence? This economic, social, and cultural evolution has also transformed America's political discourse. Unprecedented vitriol from opposing political tribes is threatening to be accepted as the new normal within major media outlets and social media.

What makes these tribal warriors do what they do, and why should we care?

Understanding what motivates extremism is crucial to those of us who believe that this resurgence of tribalism foments more divisiveness in our society, obstructing the natural process of understanding each other. Understanding the reasons for this resurgent tribalism is crucial to finding cooperative solutions to our world's problems.

America's partisan extremists are not most worrisome for their ideology, but rather for their anger. They are frightened, confused, and angry individuals who band together in tribal organizations to find physical, intellectual, and emotional security. They are Republicans, Democrats, and Independents. They are men and women, young and old.

While there is a far greater number of people in our modern world who are not violent, many share the fears of the more extreme. They also share an affection for absolutism, seeing things as 100 percent one way, black and white, making them more difficult to appeal to with facts. They ridicule the news media that presents information and opinion that challenge their worldview and profess certainty that the counter view is un-American and a danger to themselves or others.

We see it in our electoral politics, as people cluster more and more with people like them. Thirty years ago, only 20 percent of Americans lived in communities in which the presidential candidate of their party carried their congressional district by twenty or more percentage points (a landslide). Today nearly 50 percent of Americans live in such ideologically secluded communities.[12] We saw this in stark relief during the 2016 American presidential race, which was the most divisive and vitriolic in 150 years.

This partisan segregation blocks the opportunity for greater understanding of the opposing tribe, begetting further separation, misunderstanding, and animosity. Increasingly these politically segregated neighborhoods are becoming hyper-partisan political fortresses—where tribal members inhale their own ideological oxygen, seal themselves off from alternative views, and fortify their positions with fake news and conspiracy theories.

While empathy can help us better understand our neighbors and lead to reconciling our differences, modern tribalism represents a continuing real and present danger to that reconciliation.

12 David Wasserman and Ally Flinn, "Introducing the 2017 Cook Political Report Partisan Voter Index," April 7, 2017, https://cookpolitical.com/introducing-2017-cook -political-report-partisan-voter-index.

Chapter Seven

Empathy Strikes Back

If it happens again, everyone will do the exact same thing:
We will help.
—Stratis Valamios[1]

The island of Lesbos, surrounded by the beautiful blue-green Aegean Sea, evokes ancient tales of Greek adventure and modern fantasies of idyllic vacations far from the problems and stress of modern life.

But Lesbos is far more than a tourist getaway. In 2015 its ordinary people demonstrated extraordinary generosity and humanity to over 500,000 desperate refugees fleeing the war in Syria. This community of shepherds, fishermen, waiters, and housekeepers turned their island and their lives upside-down to come to the rescue of thousands of families tossed upon the sea in frail boats.

The people of Lesbos received ten times as many refugees as the entire United States only reluctantly agreed to admit. The people of Lesbos were no less frightened by this influx of refugees than were Americans, British, or Hungarians, and nowhere near as well equipped to help them. But they did it anyway.

When thousands of refugees began arriving on the small island, a Lesbos shepherd, Yorgos Sofianis, described it this way to a *New York Times* reporter: "At first even my sheep were scared because of all of the screams. But, like us, they got used to it."[2]

---

1   Liz Alderman, "Greek Villagers Rescued Migrants. Now They Are the Ones Suffering," *New York Times,* August 17, 2016, https://www.nytimes.com/2016/08/18/world/europe/greece-lesbos-refugees.html.
2   Alderman, "Greek Villagers Rescued Migrants."

The conflict in Syria, which began as a flight to freedom by its citizens against Syria's genocidal president, Bashar al-Assad, exploded into a confused, multisided struggle for survival. The country became a cauldron of violence amid the Syrian army and their chemical weapons, Iran's cruel Hezbollah fighters, Russia's massive indiscriminate bombing, ISIS's savage terrorism, and America's destruction of cities infected with ISIS fighters.

The result was total destruction, a humanitarian nightmare in which thousands of men, women, and children were slaughtered every week. Major cities such as Homs, Syria's second largest, were reduced to rubble. Millions of Syrians fled to save their families with just what they could carry on their backs, first overland to neighbor Turkey and then by frail boats to Europe.

The tiny Greek island of Lesbos was the nearest safe harbor.

Day after day, for months, the humble people of Lesbos turned their fishing boats into makeshift rescue craft, while scores of others provided emergency medical care, warm clothes, and shelter to those pulled from the sea. The magnitude of 500,000 men, women, and children staggering in from the sea is difficult to imagine. The number of discarded life preservers alone produced a mountain twenty feet high and one hundred yards long.

In all hours of the day and night, the desperate kept coming, overwhelming the island and its meager resources. But the people of Lesbos also kept coming, leaving their stores, their farms, their homes, and their families to tend to those thrown up on their shore—babies, thousands of babies, and their desperate parents.

One fisherman, Stratis Valamios, took his boat over a mile out to sea to meet a refugee armada headed toward his small town of Skala Sikamineas: "I'd be in the middle of the sea, and I would see 50 boats zigzagging toward me....I would speed toward them, and they would throw their children into my boat to be saved."[3]

When he arrived on the beach that night with his cargo of humanity, Valamios was met by over one hundred people from his village

---

3   Alderman, "Greek Villagers Rescued Migrants."

who had come to help the wet, cold, and hungry refugees. Theano Laoumis, who works at a tavern, summed it up: "The whole village is proud of what we did....You didn't know who to save first, there were so many people. But we did save them. It was only natural."[4]

This was no one-week wonder; the waves of humanity went on for two years, so the village established a system for rescuing the refugees in their struggling, waterlogged boats. Spotters on the beach would look for the overloaded boats and then call to the fishermen to race out to meet them before the boats sank and more people drowned. The people on shore brought them to their homes and gave them dry clothes and milk for their babies.

Imagine thousands of bedraggled strangers arriving at your door in the middle of the night. Frightening to be sure. Yet the people of Lesbos took them in and shared what they had. They overcame their fears and stood together to face this tsunami of thousands of strangers—people of different languages, cultures, and religions.

The profound generosity of the simple people of Lesbos is all the more stunning when viewed within the same prism as the images in Europe and America—animated anti-immigrant demonstrators, faces distorted in angry epithets thrown at bewildered refugees, and national leaders exploiting that anger for political advantage.

What we see in the faces of those demonstrators is fear of "hordes" of bedraggled "others" who threatened their safety, their livelihoods, and the homogeneity of their communities. But why did the people of Lesbos see these same bedraggled refugees as victims in need of their aid?

Why did they risk so much for these desperate strangers whom they did not know and who, in their enormous numbers, posed a genuine threat to their small island? Their hearts went out to these people as if they were family.

Lesbos is not a wealthy island; the people get by as they have for years, fishing, herding, and serving tourists. The deluge of refugees devastated their economy, with tourism down 80 percent a year later.

---

4   Alderman, "Greek Villagers Rescued Migrants."

The people of Lesbos paid a heavy price for their generosity, and the island has yet to recover. Still, Valamios the fisherman is not bitter, nor does he harbor regrets: "If it happens again, everyone will do the exact same thing: We will help."[5]

We have much to learn from the people of Lesbos. This tiny island may well represent the highest concentration of genuine heroes in the world. But where did they find the courage? What made them all act so selflessly? What sustained their extraordinary generosity?

To put this in some perspective, President Obama was harshly criticized when he suggested that America should respond to this humanitarian crisis by raising our quotas on refugees and accept fifty thousand people. Fifty thousand—less than one-tenth of the number welcomed by the tiny island of Lesbos! One-twentieth of what Germany accepted. President Trump proposed cutting that number at least in half and limiting the grounds for claiming asylum in America. When he announced his candidacy for president, Donald Trump used as his central theme the false claim that Mexican immigrants were a serious threat to American security.

The fear of refugees in America has reached a fever pitch: *They might be terrorists. They don't speak English. Most of them are Muslim. They might be criminals.* These fears burst into American life despite the existing, intense two-year screening process required of immigrants to enter this country. The fear in America has grown so intense, as opportunist politicians exploit a long-standing American ambivalence about immigration, that rational discussion about immigration seems impossible.

Of course, the citizens of Lesbos surely felt many of the same fears, but they did not recoil; they embraced their struggling fellow human beings.

In reading the accounts of the Lesbos rescue, one cannot help but be struck by the comments of the villagers.

"We had to do something."

"It was only natural."

---

5   Alderman, "Greek Villagers Rescued Migrants."

"People who couldn't swim would sink to the bottom like a stone."
"The babies, so many babies."[6]

The accounts are most often about the suffering of the individual men, women, and children they saw up close: a small, lifeless baby; the struggling mother who couldn't swim and sank beneath the waves; the nearly universal look of total exhaustion and despair on the faces of people who had suffered first war and now homelessness.

The Greek people are known for their warmth and generosity; still, the Lesbos rescue required far more than cultural kindness and hospitality. That rescue story is replete with not only hundreds of individual examples of heroism but also hundreds of everyday people banding together in extraordinary acts of generosity—sustained over several years.

How did the people of Lesbos find their empathy for immigrants in dire need when so many others in larger, wealthier societies could not find theirs?

One can only imagine that in the case of the people of Lesbos, faced with the suffering of literally hundreds of thousands, their mirror neurons must have been exploding with a flood of emotions. Their empathy was palpable, individually and as a community. Most exciting, their capacity to feel what the refugees felt and act on those feelings is an example of humanity's great potential—an entire community acting as one to come to the aid of strangers who needed help.

Perhaps that is one of the central lessons from Lesbos: none of us is truly a stranger or of a different tribe; we are all connected; we are all one. We feel what they feel, and we can act on those feelings. Unlike so many other people around the world who turned their backs on this flood of refugees, the people of Lesbos did not look away or say it was someone else's problem. Sure, the problem landed in their laps, but that is also true in America and Western Europe. Perhaps one explanation for their heroics is a product of their culture and heritage.

If deliberate awareness is important to engaging our empathy, perhaps islanders learn that "eyes open" awareness of the sea was

---

6 Alderman, "Greek Villagers Rescued Migrants."

essential to survival, since the sea can hold peril as well as bounty. And, perhaps, their depth of empathy for strangers reflects generations of being exposed to newcomers to their island, which sits at the nexus of Africa, Asia, and Europe.

Social research suggests, and North Carolina community organizer Rick Riddick proved with C. P. Ellis and Ann Atwater, that enough exposure to difference can create a sense of normalcy and less perceived threat from that difference.

But it also seems that another important dynamic must have been at work in the mobilization of entire villages to take altruistic action together to help people in trouble: empathic contagion.

Most of us probably have a sense that fear, the flipside of empathy, is contagious. It is an essential element in mob violence, which has been studied and dramatized in American culture for generations. Literature like *To Kill a Mockingbird* and classic films like *Twelve Angry Men* and *The Ox-Bow Incident* exposed the raw, emotional nerve of mob psychology.

That contagion clearly played a role in the lynching of Blacks in the South and the merciless beating of white truck driver Reginald Denny during the LA riots in 1992. Also, we know of the panic created by someone yelling "gun" in a theater, concert, or airport as frightened mobs trample others in their desperate race for safety.

Investigations of these incidents often reveal that most of the participants didn't know why they were running, just that others were running, screaming, and clearly in great panic, so they ran in panic as well. The same is true of mob violence, which seems to infect bystanders at riots, demonstrations, and even political rallies, as individuals succumb to the virus and become participants.

The mountains of studies done on Nazi Germany have confirmed that when we witness others who are frightened, fearful, or even violent, we feel a primordial connection with those feelings of others—a mirroring of those feelings. This is additional evidence that humans are born prewired with an innate alertness to danger, which can be triggered by fear of people who are different. Nazi propagandist Joseph Goebbels was diabolically brilliant in portraying people not of Aryan blood as dangerous, evil, and even subhuman.

Once target groups had been "othered," from there it was a relatively short leap to convincing Germans that these dangerous people were deserving of contempt, then condemnation, and finally, elimination from the German tribe. To succeed in enlisting millions of otherwise decent human beings to do very inhuman things required the conversion of that broadly felt fear to hatred and then to violence. But it starts with fear.

The Nazis orchestrated events such as the Reichstag fire, Kristallnacht, and patriotic torch light rallies using a constant flow of anti-Semitic rhetoric to incubate this contagion of fear into suspicion, resentment, and eventually, hatred.

Goebbels mined the very worst of humanity. But did Lesbos prove that we can also mine empathy, the best of humanity? When an office colleague bursts into tears at the news that she has lost her job, and first one and then another and another colleague race to her side to console her, isn't that contagious empathy?

If empathy can be contagious, it could become a powerful antidote to mass fear. But is it contagious, and how can we encourage the contagion?

To answer these questions, we need to consider the act of yawning. At some point most of us have found it impossible to stifle a yawn in response to a friend's yawn. This simple act has led to a great deal of research into whether this response and other emotional responses are coincidence, mimicry, or contagion.

That was the subject of work done by yet two more Italian neuroscientists, this time in Pisa, Italy. What is it with Italians and empathy? Elisabetta Palagi, Ivan Norscia, and Elisa Demuru used yawn contagion in humans and apes to test emotional contagion in general and empathy in particular.

Their findings support the recent discovery of mirror neurons, which we discussed in an earlier chapter. In their studies, when humans or apes (in this instance, bonobos) witnessed another of their species yawning, they often had the emotional response of unconscious mimicry—particularly among kin or close friends. Palagi, Norscia, and Demuru reported: "In humans and apes, yawn contagion echoes emotional contagion, the basal layer of empathy. Hence, yawn contagion is a unique tool to compare to empathy across species."[7]

Interestingly, they also discovered that this mirrored emotional response was strongest among family members, next strongest among close friends, and weakest among those well outside the familial group. Again, we find that our emotional connection, and therefore our empathy, is strongest among our closest tribal members and weakens as people become less familiar.

We can hypothesize that the extraordinary outpouring of mass empathy toward the refugees lucky enough to land in Lesbos was at least aided by the fact that it was a small, close-knit community of family and friends who readily welcomed visitors into their "family." This is not to diminish the remarkable generosity and heroics of the rescuers in Lesbos, but rather to recognize what the Italian researchers hypothesized: the closer the social bonds, the greater the likelihood of empathy between people.

If we want more empathy in the world, we need to understand the mechanism that allows social bonds or familiarity to serve as a pathway to empathy and then build on it.

Nearly two hundred years ago, Austrian psychological theorist Alfred Adler wrote about what he called "social interest." He suggested that we all have the innate ability to feel for others and that contributing to the common good is an imperative that differentiates the "healthy from the unhealthy, the functional from the dysfunctional," as psychotherapist Liza Finlay described it.[8]

Adler was suggesting that helping others, or having social interest, was not only an act of generosity but also an act of individual and community wellness. However, he also made clear that this capacity for social interest must be nurtured and developed.

---

7   Elisabetta Palagi, Ivan Norscia, and Elisa Demuru, "Yawn Contagion in Humans and Bonobos: Emotional Affinity Matters More than Species." *PeerJ* (August 2012), https://peerj.com/articles/519/.

8   Liza Finlay, "Turns Out Empathy Is Contagious," *HuffPost*, November 30, 2012, http://www.huffingtonpost.ca/liza-finlay/teaching-kids-empathy_b_2220570.html.

So, empathy can be contagious and, in a sense, can be harnessed by individuals of goodwill to improve the qualities of their lives and the world around them. It can be used as a force for good against the resurgence of tribal fear and hatred.

The strategy for using empathy to "fight back" might not be to refute tribal fears but rather to use our empathic power to better understand those fears and use that understanding to begin to bridge tribal divisions, erode tribal walls, and as a result, reduce conflict.

Bridging divisions requires a degree of self-reflection or perspective, in which we consider the personal experiences that might have shaped the other person's point of view, what biases and assumptions we bring to the table, and where might we start to find shared values or perspectives.

Beyond the island of Lesbos, empathy is eroding tribal walls on other fronts as well...and in some extraordinary ways. In North Carolina, Martin Luther King Jr. disciple and civil rights activist Reverend William J. Barber II teamed up with former conservative Republican and former New Moral Majority member Jonathan Wilson-Hartgrove to bridge divisions in America. Another odd couple to be sure.

Barber's movement, called the Poor People's Campaign: A National Call for a Moral Revival (an update of Dr. King's Poor People's Campaign), moves from town to town telling the story of how America became so divided and describing what is necessary for us to begin to come together. Barber and Wilson-Hartgrove share the conviction that to reconnect we need to better understand each other and embrace the many central, moral issues that unite us in common cause, broadening our awareness beyond the parochial issues of the day.

Barber and Wilson-Hartgrove argue that America's current political divisions are not natural, that they are the result of contrived political strategies designed to win votes by dividing Americans and pitting one group against another—Blacks against whites, rich against poor, Christians against Muslims.

In fact, Barber and Wilson-Hartgrove joined forces to write a book on bridging those divides: *The Third Reconstruction: How a Moral Movement*

Is Overcoming the Politics of Division and Fear. They understand that fear is the deep, underlying driver of the tragic divisiveness we see play out every day in America, and their unlikely partnership is devoted to telling the story of how understanding the "other person" is central to healing.[9]

In Chicago, Rami Nashashibi, a Muslim whose family came from Jordan, grew up in an American city where anger and violence had been gradually escalating. Much of that violence centered around street gangs and between different racial and ethnic groups. Rami watched with alarm as tensions spread to Muslim shopkeepers and their Black customers.

He could see that the tension came from cultural misunderstandings of each other's motives, allowing suspicion and resentment to grow. Were the shopkeepers trying to gouge their Black customers, and did the inner-city youth pose a threat of robbery?

Rami had the awareness to clearly see the reasons for mutual suspicion among people on both sides of his beloved community, and it broke his heart. He experienced feelings of exclusion and bias from members of both tribes. With some perspective, he found an answer.

His solution was novel, but simple. He created ways in which Muslims could show South Side Black residents that they understood their concerns and cared enough to do something about them. Rami created the Inner-City Muslim Action Network (IMAN), organizing concerned Muslims interested in closing the growing gap between Muslims and non-Muslims in the local community.

Since there are very few supermarkets with substantial buying power in inner cities, there is little availability of perishable, healthy, fresh fruits and vegetables. As a result, many Blacks assumed that the small, local shop owners didn't care about their customers' health, while the shop owners assumed that there was insufficient local consumer demand for them to make the substantial investment to provide those healthy foods.

---

9   William Barber and Jonathan Wilson-Hartgrove, "Rev. William Barber Is Building a New 'Moral Movement' to Reach People on Race," interview by Charlayne Hunter-Gault, *PBS NewsHour*, June 23, 2017, https://www.pbs.org/newshour/show/rev-william-barber-building-new-moral-movement-reach-people-race.

The local Chicago community's fear and suspicion of this influx of Muslim immigrant shop owners grew and began to develop into resentment, with the "evidence" of the absence of nutritious and affordably priced produce demonstrating that the shop owners cared little about the needs of the community. The suspicion of the local community presented itself as "unfriendly" to the shop owners, who became fearful and suspicious themselves, particularly of the intentions of the young African American men. Both sides harbored fear, both had blind biases, and both had "evidence" that the members of the other tribe meant them harm. Tribal walls began to rise and empathy to recede.

Rami understood the suspicions of both sides, and IMAN launched a program in which local nonprofits helped subsidize the acquisition of fresh fruits and vegetables by local food marts and encouraged their purchase by the community through health information mini-fairs. Rami and his volunteers would be present at the food marts, giving free tastings of fruit and vegetable dishes, complete with information on their preparation and health benefits, and they did it with a smile, a laugh, and often a hug.

The feeling that tribal walls and suspicion were melting away was palpable. Soon, the food marts became a place that connected people within a community that had been growing more and more disconnected and adversarial.

Also, in an effort to improve the health of the local community, IMAN recruited Muslim medical staff in Chicago to provide free services to low-income Chicago residents who lacked access to health care. The scene of a young female Muslim physician's assistant wearing a hijab and tending to the injuries of a large African American man could bring tears to your eyes.

The message at both the food marts and the free clinics was "We are neighbors, we understand and share the challenges that you face in our community, and we seek to bridge our cultural and racial differences." The message from the African American community was "Thank you for kindness, for understanding the challenges we face, and for reaching out to us; you have won our trust." This was the source of the hugs.

Awareness of the struggles of each other and the empathy to feel the concerns of each other brought these groups together, broke down tribal suspicions and biases, led to better understanding, and eventually resolved differences. It was not everything that the community needed, but it was a start.

As a result of this success in South Chicago, Rami is taking these programs to other American cities, encouraging greater understanding and bridging divides.[10]

For generations, humanity has been flirting with empathy and its remarkable potential for good, but never collectively seizing that potential to change the world. In a world wracked by violence, empathy is a healing force.

The people of Lesbos, Barber and Wilson-Hartgrove, and Rami Nashashibi didn't need a social psychologist to tell them this; they each in their own way called on their empathy. This is one contagion worth propagating.

---

10 Rami Nashashibi, "Rebuilding a Chicago Neighborhood by Forging Connections to the Muslim Community," interview by Jeffrey Brown, *PBS NewsHour*, June 23, 2017, https://www.pbs.org /newshour/show/rebuilding-chicago-neighborhood-forging-connections-muslim-community.

Chapter Eight

Head and Heart

Compassion hurts. When you feel connected to everything, you also feel responsible for everything. And you cannot turn away. Your destiny is bound with the destinies of others. You must either learn to carry the Universe or be crushed by it.
—Andrew Boyd[1]

A common question running throughout this book is, Why do ordinary people step out of their everyday lives to do extraordinary acts of kindness and generosity—acts of heroism, really? Along the way I have proposed some answers, using science, politics, and history as support.

In this chapter I introduce you to someone who has taken human empathy as far as it seemingly can go. In so doing we can examine the healthy limits of empathy and consider strategies that might serve to guide empathy for maximum positive impact for those around us and for ourselves.

Mohamed and Dawn Bzeek are anything but ordinary, and the extraordinary nature of their deeds required such a level of personal sacrifice that their story stands apart. Their story explores the outer boundaries of empathy and also serves as a cautionary tale.

Dawn died a few years ago, but just recently Mohamed's story was "discovered" by the media and the outpouring of support for him was a lesson in itself. Despite the divisiveness and tribalism that

---

1 Andrew Boyd, *Daily Afflictions: The Agony of Being Connected to Everything in the Universe* (New York: W. W. Norton, 2002).

has dominated the news media over the past few years, the Bzeeks' story generated intense interest and unqualified praise across the deep fissures in America.

Mohamed is a Muslim immigrant who succeeded in transcending the suspicion and bias of his ethnic and cultural differences with a unifying story that uplifts and inspires as it challenges our capacity to comprehend such generosity of spirit.

As a college student in Libya, Mohamed was a marathon runner who traveled to the US in the late 1970s to study engineering. He became a US citizen in 1997, eight years after marrying Dawn, who was already quite extraordinary in her own right as a foster parent of children with serious illnesses. She used her home as an emergency shelter for children who needed foster care or were placed in protective services.

Upon meeting Dawn and seeing what she faced, rather than being overwhelmed, Mohamed dove right in. The two were foster parents in the Los Angeles area to kids with severe special needs, taking on the most heart-wrenching cases. They lectured at the local community college on caring and grieving for kids with life-threatening conditions and served on state task forces for improving foster care.

Their work as foster parents and advocates for needy children would be more than enough "good works" for a lifetime for most of us, but not for the Bzeeks, who seemed to have an unlimited capacity for personal sacrifice. People in the community came to them with stories of more and more very young children who desperately needed their love and attention—the most difficult and heart-wrenching challenges.

The Bzeeks chose the cases that no one else would take, such as terminally ill young children with "do not resuscitate" orders. The idea that these kids would die alone in an impersonal hospital ward was too much for Mohamed and Dawn to accept. They would be there for these kids, regardless of what it might require of them. In a PBS interview, Mohamed succinctly described the indescribable: "To me, death is part of life. And I'm glad that I help these kids go through this period of time, you know? And I help him. I be with him. I comfort him. I love him or her. And until he passes away, I am with him and make him feel he has family and he have somebody who cares about him and loves him."[2]

When Dawn died in 2015, Mohamed carried on by himself, sixty-two years old and alone. A large bear of a man, with a full beard, soft voice, and disarming smile, Mohamed had found his calling, and he wasn't about to stop.[3]

Like most of us, Mohamed had his own life to live, a career to manage, groceries to buy, a house to maintain, and bills to pay. He enjoyed the little time off he could scratch out of a day, watching sports and visiting friends. Nevertheless, when people at the local hospital or from social services called to ask if he could take in yet another child whom no one else could manage, he almost always said of course.

With the limited, part-time assistance of a nurse who helps out on weekends, Mohamed is now the sole caregiver to the most severely ill children. One is a little girl born with microcephaly, a rare disorder in which the baby's brain does not fully develop, a condition publicized in the 2010s due to the outbreak of the Zika virus. It is nearly always fatal and totally disabling.

Mohamed's little girl is now six and has been with him since she was one month old. She cannot hear or see and responds only to touch. At seven weeks, the child's biological parents couldn't care for her, so the county called Bzeek. Mohamed sleeps on a couch next to her every night, takes her to the hospital for regular appointments, and argues with insurance companies. Most importantly, he is with her day and night, and when he puts his face next to her, she can feel his presence—it makes her smile.

Hard, very hard. But Mohamed described it this way: "I know it's a heartbreak. I know it's a lot of work. I know it's going to hurt me sometimes. You know, I feel sad. But, in my opinion, we should help each other, you know?"[4]

---

2   Mohamed Bzeek, "The Foster Father Who Cares When Terminally Ill Kids Have No One," interview by Gayle Tzemach Lemmon, *PBS NewsHour*, February 24, 2017, https://www .pbs.org/newshour/show/foster-father-cares-terminally-ill-kids-no-one.
3   Bzeek, "The Foster Father Who Cares."
4   Bzeek, "The Foster Father Who Cares."

Children come and go through Mohamed's home, some living only a few months, one dying so young that Mohamed sought out a doll maker to create an outfit for her funeral.

To most of us, the burden that Mohamed carries is almost unimaginable. But on top of all of that, Mohamed is also caring for his biological son, Adam, who was born in 1997 with brittle bone disease and dwarfism, so fragile as a child that changing his diapers or his socks could break his bones.

Mohamed has loved and nurtured Adam day after day, week after week, year after year. Now nineteen, Adam weighs just sixty-five pounds. He drives a wheelchair to class at Citrus College. Given all the good that he does, Mohamed could be forgiven if he were bitter about his son's disabilities. But he's not. He views his son as a precious gift and loves him with all of his very sizable heart, saying, "That's the way God created him."[5]

In November 2016, Mohamed's story began to evoke the biblical story of Job when this big, strong man was diagnosed with colon cancer. The doctor told him that they would need to operate soon, to which Mohamed pleaded, "Doctor, I can't. You have to give me time because I have a foster kid who is terminal. And I have a son. He is handicapped. There is nobody for them, you now?" In December he drove to the hospital for his surgery alone. But it went well, and his prognosis is good. And with the help of a part-time nurse's aide, he carries on.

Recently, a GoFundMe fundraising site was set up for Mohamed and his precious little children, and the outpouring of money and supporting comments has been miraculous. He has read every note. He said, "Every day I was crying because of their kindness and the nice words they said."[6] He now had the funds to repair a leaky roof and replace his fourteen-year-old van. He carries on.

Mohamed's wife, Dawn, made him aware of the sad reality that our world includes very young children with profoundly tragic medical

5   Bzeek, "The Foster Father Who Cares."
6   Bzeek, "The Foster Father Who Cares."

conditions who must face the remainder of their short lives alone, without family or friends to comfort them.

That awareness opened the door to his extraordinary empathy for these children, which he describes so well: "And until he passes away, I am with him and make him feel he has family, and he has somebody who cares about him and loves him."[7] Mohamed feels what they feel.

Of course, what makes the case of the Bzeeks particularly extraordinary is that they devoted their lives to the 24-hour-a-day job of caring for, worrying about, holding, and grieving for several dozen kids with no letup and, until recently, very little support or recognition. He gave everything that he had for kids who were all strangers to him when he met them.

As remarkable as is their story, a closer look at Mohamed and Dawn provides all of the explanation we need to understand how they found the empathy for these kids where others looked away. It is clear from their actions that Mohamed and Dawn lived their lives with exceptionally acute awareness of the suffering around them, seeking out children with extreme medical conditions. Their empathy for children suffering alone seemed boundless because they couldn't say no. Their altruism in taking the children into their homes to live with them until they died is an act of such grace that it is almost unimaginable to most of us.

But at the same time, Mohamed's response to his feelings of empathy and his degree of personal sacrifice for these children was all-consuming, like Mother Teresa, and well beyond what even the most empathic among us would consider. So, what are we to make of this? Is it the standard of empathic love to which we should each hold ourselves?

I have included the Bzeeks' story not just because it is uplifting but also because it is very painful to read. This story raises difficult questions about the limits of the human capacity to live a healthy, productive life and still follow the dictates of an empathic heart. Some people might say that this extreme empathy is unhealthy or

---

7   Bzeek, "The Foster Father Who Cares."

counterproductive. In fact, some people who have studied empathy say just that—that it can be excessive. Paul Bloom, professor of psychology and cognitive science at Yale University, wrote a book titled *Against Empathy*.[8]

Despite the provocative title, Bloom makes clear in his book that he is *not* against empathy. In fact, he believes it is of great value to society. Rather, he is concerned that empathy can become too all-consuming and counterproductive, even undermining the purpose of one's compassion. Additionally, he takes exception to what he sees as the overpopularizing of empathy as a cure-all for the world's problems. Not surprisingly, the subtitle for *Against Empathy* is *The Case for Rational Compassion*, arguing for the use of reason to modulate and direct one's empathy.

Earlier in this book I briefly discussed the importance of reason to provide us with perspective and ensure that our empathy is applied to do the most good. Bloom reminds us that reason's role should merit more than a passing reference.

The case of Mohamed Bzeek highlights at least one of Bloom's concerns. He uses the term *spotlight* as a descriptor for the phenomenon in which well-intentioned people or organizations focus on the plight of a single individual to the exclusion of other similarly needy people, redirecting the attention of society away from the plight of the larger group.

Bloom is also concerned that another casualty of that redirection can be justice. Combating institutional injustice or systemic need is often less compelling than responding to the single act of suffering to which it is easier to relate. People who share this concern might argue that when a charity spotlights a single individual's plight, such as the GoFundMe focus on Bzeek's little girl with microcephaly, the community responds overwhelmingly to that single child rather than spreading out their generosity, giving some of that support to other needy kids.

Bloom posits that in extreme cases unfettered empathy can produce an excessive response or a less helpful response—for example, when

---

8   Paul Bloom, *Against Empathy: The Case for Rational Compassion* (New York: Ecco, 2016).

a much-publicized flood disaster leads to thousands of well-meaning people sending tons of clothing and perishable food even though the relief organizations could have put cash donations to better use.

I cite Professor Bloom's concerns because it is another side of this subject that is worth discussing. Further, I agree with Bloom that with a little detached perspective, empathy can be directed to make altruism more effective.

At the same time, I disagree that empathy and altruism are part of a zero-sum response requiring that we husband our caring resources and do cost-benefit calculations on our generosity. I don't think that it works that way.

It might be true that in some instances, donors' attention can be redirected from the larger cause to the needs of a few individuals. However, there is a great deal of data on the behavior of volunteers and donors that suggests that generosity is *not* a zero-sum game, in which an increase in giving to one cause triggers an equal reduction in the amount to another. Rather, an emergency need for additional support, such as the dislocation of people following a hurricane, tends to reliably increase the total funds donated to the larger cause of disaster relief. Awareness of need encourages altruism, which breeds further altruism.

Nevertheless, Bloom has raised some important questions about where reason fits into the role of empathy. In *Against Empathy*, Bloom cites a 1995 study published in the *Journal of Personality and Social Psychology*, which focused on altruism, using a fictitious dying child and charity in an experiment. As explained in Bloom's book, a team of psychologists described to the study's participants a charity that invested in quality of life for terminally ill children. The participants would then listen to an interview of a potential applicant seeking financial support from the charity.

Participants were split in two groups. One group was instructed to "try to take an objective perspective toward what is described. Try not to get caught up in how the child who is interviewed feels;

just remain objective and detached."[9] The other group was told to prepare for the interview by trying to "imagine how the child who is interviewed feels about what has happened and how it has affected this child's life. Try to feel the full impact of what this child has been through and how he or she feels as a result." Bloom called these the low-empathy and high-empathy contexts.[10]

Both participant groups listened to an interview with a very brave, bright 10-year-old applicant, who described her painful illness. Following the interview, researchers asked participants if they would choose to advance the little girl's place on the charity's list for funding. The experiment's subjects were told that if this applicant were designated a priority, other sick children would wait a longer time for support for their quality of life. Bloom wrote: "The effect was strong. Three-quarters of the subjects in the high-empathy condition wanted to move her up, as compared to one-third in the low-empathy condition. Empathy's effects, then, weren't in the direction of increasing an interest in justice. Rather, they increased special concern for the target of the empathy, despite the cost to others."[11]

From this study, you can see why Bloom has his concerns: humans tend to personalize things.[12]

In certain circumstances that tendency to personalize is an empathic response that favors those closest to us, which could unwittingly run counter to the larger objectives of the altruism. Hence the need for rational intervention. Bloom articulates his case for "rational compassion" this way: "I want to make a case for the value of conscious, deliberative reasoning in everyday life, arguing that we should strive to use our heads rather than our hearts."[13]

I agree with Bloom on the importance of managing our empathy, not losing ourselves in feeling what others feel, and using our heads in deciding how we act upon our empathy. Further, I share the concern

---

9   Bloom, *Against Empathy*, 86.
10 Bloom, *Against Empathy*, 86.
11 Bloom, *Against Empathy*, 86.
12 See also Jesse Singal, "Why Empathy Is Bad," *New York Magazine*, December 28, 2016.
13 Bloom, *Against Empathy*, 5.

of some criminal justice experts who have expressed that with the increased attention in courts to victim statements and the details of their individual suffering, vengeance could take center stage rather than dispassionate justice and the rule of law.

At the same time, Bloom's statement that "we should strive to use our heads rather than our hearts" implies what I view as a false choice: either-or.

Empathy should be guided by reason but not replaced by it. For a rational, humane society to function we need both: our emotions (empathy) to fully understand what the "other guy" feels and our intellect (cognitive perspective) to manage our action, to ensure that it is effective and well directed.

I have some concerns about possible unintended consequences from accepting this false choice between an emotional or cognitive response. For example, Bloom's admonition that to "use our heads rather than our hearts" could provide "permission" for those feeling ambivalent to walk past someone in need, or to be less patient with another point of view, or to accept half measures in their altruism.

Accepting the false choice of head or heart can inhibit an important element of the complex mix that ensures our humanity, in which we eschew the purely rational response and instead demonstrate simply that we care. *I knew that giving $100 was probably more than we could afford at the time, but I felt it was the right thing to do. Or, I probably wasted my time trying again to understand his argument, but I couldn't just walk away from him.*

Further, sometimes we employ a sound, rational argument to serve as a rationalization for inaction, such as: *He will probably just spend it on alcohol. I have more important things to do than listen to him. Her views are so extreme, it's not worth my effort to come halfway.*

Engaging our reason, taking perspective, is an important governor of our empathy. But I worry that unless reason's role as a guide is clearly understood, it will become a convenient excuse to turn off the pleadings of our empathy when they are inconvenient.

Empathy is not the answer to all of the world's problems, but it could be a crucial starting point if it is guided by reason.

Empathy can be an antidote to fear of people who are different, an enticement to draw people out of the safety of their exclusive tribes, and a reminder of why we need to be patient to better understand where the other person is coming from and to encourage us to listen to divergent views. Often these acts require empathy's nudge for us to leave our comfort zone as spectators and act.

A balanced approach to empathy includes being deliberately aware of the world around us, the painful as well as the uplifting; opening our hearts to feel what others feel; applying reason or perspective in directing those feelings; and acting when and where we deem appropriate.

Chapter Nine

Awareness to Action

Whatever there is of God and goodness in the universe,
it must work itself out and express itself through us.
We cannot stand aside and let God do it.
—Albert Einstein[1]

The extraordinary stories of empathy in the preceding chapters are certainly inspiring. But they beg an essential question: How can we collectively and individually harness empathy to reduce the divisiveness and conflict in our world today?

More specifically, how do we evolve a diverse America—of many races, ethnicities, cultures, sexual orientations, and opinions—into a single nation of shared values and aspirations? How do we restore understanding, comity, and respect across tribal lines? How do we learn to transcend our differences to knit together a community of acceptance and trust? And how do we learn to open our eyes and our minds to understand the challenges and pain that others feel?

While there are no simple answers, we have seen how the power of empathy can address all of these difficult questions.

During the height of the pandemic, we saw hundreds of examples of health workers and first responders going well beyond their professional duty, fighting for a little humanity in the midst of the suffering. Some exhausted and overstressed nurses held cell phones

---

1   Alice Calaprice, ed., *The Ultimate Quotable Einstein* (Princeton, NJ: Princeton University Press, 2013).

to the ears of their dying, quarantined patients so that in their last moments they might hear their family's loving words.

Even during the heated and chaotic moments of the demonstrations following the killing of George Floyd, we saw instances of police and marchers taking a knee together in human solidarity. When looters and rioters exploited the demonstrations by destroying local businesses in several cities, they were followed the next day by hundreds of community volunteers with brooms and shovels, sweeping up the damage and beginning repairs.

In this chapter I have attempted to formalize an approach to harnessing our empathy for the common good. In the final chapter I recommend specific steps to help us as a society and as individuals apply that approach to both large-scale social problems and everyday challenges.

This approach to harnessing our empathy rests on scientific research with humans and other mammals, plus "experiments in the field" by courageous people such as Nicholas Winton, John Howard Griffin, Natalie Hampton, C. P. Ellis, Mohamed and Dawn Bzeek, and the residents of Lesbos.

I studied these cases and dozens of others in an effort to understand the roots of modern tribalism and to identify the mechanism that engages empathy to encourage altruism during times of raw division. The reason I picked such varied examples of empathy was to demonstrate how ordinary people, not lifetime crusaders or social welfare professionals, were inspired to find their empathy to produce remarkable outcomes.

I was just an observer, a person who connected the dots on what we might learn from science, politics, and personal experiences about tribal fear and empathy. The MRI studies, the work of Yale's Baby Lab, the discoveries of the Italian Fab Four, and the extraordinary insights of biologists and primatologists like Frans de Waal provided the scientific foundation on which my conclusions and recommendations are based.

My approach to harnessing and propagating empathy is the sum of four central conclusions.

First, empathy is not some fanciful notion or philosophical construction. Rather, empathy consists of physical mirror neurons that have evolved in the human brain (and the brains of some other mammals) for a purpose.

Second, empathy is not sympathy or like any other emotion. It is a unique reaction that permits humans to mirror the feelings or experiences of others, placing us in the other person's shoes. As a result, empathy can lead to better understanding of others: their actions, attitudes, and beliefs—even their biases.

Third, the evidence strongly suggests that empathy, like fear, is an evolutionary response that has developed over millions of years and has stood the test of time because *it is important to the survival of our species*. It helps humans work together for our mutual survival.

Our empathic reactions to another person's suffering or differing point of view are frequently overlooked or misinterpreted because they are often inconvenient in a fast-paced modern world. To act on our empathy often demands the time to stop and help the stranded motorist, or the patience to understand why our friend holds such a different point of view. In our age, empathy might be less convenient but no less essential to our survival.

As a result, empathy could be the most underrated and underused emotion that we possess, at a time when empathy's evolutionary alter ego, primal fear, is on the rise across the globe. This is a particularly inconvenient time for empathy to be sidelined, when complex problems like climate change pose an existential threat to humanity.

Empathy is perhaps the quintessential human trait—it is what makes us a humane species, and it is surely the greatest hope for humankind.

When early hunter-gatherers struggled to find sufficient food to survive, it was likely to be empathy—understanding community needs—that made possible the collective action required for the breakthrough to agriculture. Whether the existential threat is climate change, nuclear proliferation, global pandemics, or terrorism, empathic understanding of the "other person" is crucial to finding the collective agreement necessary to address those complex, society-wide threats.

This type of cooperation plays out every day in the natural world. In discussing his remarkable book *Beyond Words: What Animals Think and Feel,* author and environmentalist Carl Safina explains: "There are documented stories of elephants finding people who were lost. In one case, an old woman who couldn't see well got lost and was found the next day with elephants guarding her. They had encased her in sort of a cage of branches to protect her from hyenas. That seems extraordinary to us, but it comes naturally to elephants."[2]

For humanity to survive, we may have to learn from other mammals. Humans complain about how difficult it is to bridge between tribes—religious, ethnic, racial, political, and more—and yet animals use their empathy to bridge between species.

My research on modern tribalism—the absolutist views, conspiracy theories, and segregation from alternative points of view—left me wondering if there was any solution to tribal conflict. Then I came across the animal studies on empathy and eventually the new science on mirror neurons that create empathy. But the clincher that empathy holds the key to addressing tribalism was the remarkable evolutionary similarity between fear and empathy, both hardwired in humans over millions of years.

That interplay between fear and empathy in the survival and progress of humanity now seems clear, and setting the right balance of that interplay could, once again, prove pivotal to the survival of our species.

This evolutionary connection of tribalism to empathy is important when you consider the primal nature of the tribal threat today. It is worth restating that only in the past few decades have we witnessed the confluence of several overlapping global events that have defined this as an historical epoch with existential implications—events that evoke primal tribal fear.

This discussion of how we address today's seemingly overwhelming challenges to a humane and united society merits restating the primal

---

2   Simon Worral, "Yes, Animals Think and Feel. Here's How We Know," *National Geographic,* July 15, 2015, 7.

nature of the fear generated by the challenges facing humanity in the twenty-first century.

Massive *global migration* in the face of ethnic and religious wars and international terrorism has flooded nations everywhere with "hordes of others" perceived as threatening national identities, social status, and economic stability. This activates the evolutionary *fear of others*.

Concurrently, accelerating *global economic change* in every corner of the world has helped fuel growing economic inequality and stagnating wages, dislocating workers and their families and making it impossible for much of the working middle class to keep up. This activates the evolutionary *fear of being left behind*.

Additionally, unprecedented *acceleration of technology and social change*—smart phones, the #MeToo movement, social media, LGBTQ rights, and artificial intelligence—have changed the face of American society from small towns to major cities. Everything seems changed, impermanent, fast, and furious. This activates the evolutionary *fear of social disruption*.

Lastly, modern media with 24/7 reach on thousands of channels, computers, tablets, and smartphones and tailored to the biases of different tribes—often designed to roil the emotions and confirm our worst fears—acts as an accelerant to the existing unstable mix, particularly in the hands of a skilled demagogue.

This is the challenge humankind faces. Even in a world of modern demagogues and sensational, partisan media, we can calm those evolutionary fears, erode the tribal walls, and begin to establish trust and mutual understanding. But it is no small task.

Which brings us back to empathy. Why is empathy the antidote, and how do we apply it? I chose to study empathy in depth because nothing else seems capable of breaching tribal walls. The research I cited earlier seems to confirm our personal experiences: more information or better information is no longer an effective inoculation against tribal fear. Conspiracy theories, alternate facts, and absolutism thrive in the medium of modern media.

People throughout the world are talking past each other, and compromise with the other tribe is considered heresy, deepening ignorance about the motivations of each other. The more I studied empathy, the more I learned that when activated, it can cut off the fuel of bigotry and bias and open a channel of understanding that can calm primal fear.

As I write these words, I am well aware that our complex modern society encourages skepticism and nihilism as antidotes to the daily cognitive dissonance that can be so troubling. From personal experience, I know that discussions of empathy as a solution to social problems can prompt vigorous eye-rolling.

Nevertheless, contemporary science and historic examples of those who have wielded empathy's power—from Gandhi to King to Mandela—provide compelling evidence that it is a profoundly powerful, if underused, human trait. If we try to focus on putting ourselves in the other person's shoes, holding back on our instinct to hit back, and instead reaching out to understand why the other person sees things as they do, it transforms the interaction from "How can you possibly believe that?" to "Tell me more. I want to understand why you feel that way."

It can, at least momentarily, break the spell of tribalism by signaling that you consider the other person's views to be important, worthy of being included in your world. A substantial driver of these tribal attitudes is the fear of not being listened to, respected, and included.

The chant of the white nationalists in Charlottesville, Virginia, told the story: "You will not replace us." The opponents to the white nationalists were not helping bridge the gap with their own chants, including "Kill all Nazis"[3] and "Punch a Nazi in the mouth."[4]

Divisiveness and hate are fueled by divisiveness and hate. Across the world, from Turkey to Venezuela to Brazil, to Hungary, to the Philippines, and finally to America, demagogic autocrats skillfully wield fear and tribalism as a political weapon.

---

3   Robert King, "Meet the Man in the Middle of the 'Unite the Right' Rally," *Indianapolis Star*, August 12, 2017, https://www.indystar.com/story/news/2017/08/12/unite-right-white-nationalist-rally-charlottesville-erupts-violence/562095001/.
4   Brian Mann, "Trump Supporter: 'He Called for Unity, I Never Saw Obama Call for Unity,'" NPR, August 14, 2017, https://www.npr.org/2017/08/14/543259485/trump-supporter-he-called-for-unity-i-never-saw-obama-call-for-unity.

When President Trump declares at campaign rallies that Mexican immigrants are rapists, gang members, and murderers, he incites fear among his supporters, then concludes with "I alone can fix it. I will restore law and order."[5]

You cannot fight fear with fear, or anger with anger; it only increases the speed of the centrifugal force spinning us away from each other.

Empathy is the countermeasure because it draws people closer to each other, in a sense, a centripetal force that connects us. As I have explained at length in earlier chapters, empathy's evolutionary design was to activate a person's mirror neurons so that they can feel what the other person feels.

In war you are taught to avoid looking into the faces of your enemy or you will humanize them, making it harder to kill. Conversely, civil rights marchers in 1950s America were taught to look directly into the eyes of the angry counter-protesters and the police, who set upon them with fists, clubs, and batons. Human eye contact engages empathy, if for but a moment.

If you see, really see, your tribal opposites, you begin to humanize them; and if you follow your empathy, you will begin to feel what they feel, which gives birth to a desire to better understand them. In one sense this is a very small step, but it represents the crucial beginning of a process that could change the tribal dynamic.

Abraham Lincoln understood this principle when he so eloquently and explicitly called on his fellow citizen's empathy at the beginning of America's most destructive tribal conflict: "We are not enemies, but friends. We must not be enemies. Though passion may have strained, it must not break our bonds of affection. The mystic chords of memory… will yet swell…when again touched, as surely, they will be, by the better angels of our nature."[6]

As Ku Klux Klan leader C. P. Ellis and Black civil rights activist Ann Atwater proved, from the seeds of understanding, almost

---

5   Yoni Appelbaum, "Only I Can Fix It," *Atlantic*, July 21, 2016, https://www.theatlantic.com /politics/archive/2016/07/trump-rnc-speech-alone-fix-it/492557/.

6   Abraham Lincoln, "First Inaugural Address," March 4, 1861, Avalon Project. http://avalon .law.yale.edu/19th_century/lincoln1.asp.

anything can grow. This brings us back to the earlier question: What's the formula for harnessing empathy, and what are the specific steps to applying that formula?

There are many ways to think about empathy and how to access it. Drawing upon the best thinking of experts on the subject, I have settled on an approach that I believe can assist us in tapping our empathy for our personal enrichment as well as for the common good. That process has four sequential elements: deliberate awareness, empathy, perspective, and action.

Deliberate awareness—of the world around us, from the person at your elbow on the subway to the person headed your way on the country path. Deliberately aware, not multitasking aware, not looking past people aware, but present in the moment, taking note of the weeping colleague, the beautiful day, the woman with her arms loaded climbing the apartment stairs. Your empathy doesn't have a chance to kick into gear if you are tuned out.

That means seeing our surroundings in a way that pierces the fog of our daily habits like texting instead of listening closely to our friend's problem; awakens us from the insensate state that permits us to walk past the lost tourist without seeing her struggle; and disrupts our world of justification that we all use to protect ourselves from getting involved in something that requires more time or courage than we feel we have at hand.

This degree of awareness requires deliberateness, to look around you and observe what's happening in your world. It has its own rewards, bringing a smile at the sight of the little girl dressed up for her first day at school, a moment of marvel at the first buds of spring, and of course, a brush with sadness for the elderly man struggling to fight off the tug of Alzheimer's. It's a mix, but if we are deliberately aware of what's happening around us, it becomes our world, a world in which we are fully alive and in which we can make our own decisions about whether to turn away or to engage.

A useful term, recently popularized, that parallels deliberate awareness is *mindfulness*—living in a state of enhanced awareness of the present. When you live in a state of mindfulness or deliberate awareness, one of your first discoveries is how much of life and the world around you had previously gone unnoticed. Life that you can reclaim. That is just one of many rewards we encounter on the path to empathy and understanding.

For most of us, without deliberate awareness we can be carried away by the day-to-day, unaware or in denial of those in our lives who need someone to walk a bit in their shoes, to feel what they feel. Awareness activates our empathy.

Being open to empathy—feeling what the other person feels. Even if you are cognitively aware of a friend's sadness or a stranger's suffering, you still need a moment to absorb what you see and let your mirror neurons translate how your friend feels. Empathy can be painful when it mirrors the feelings of the mother of the young child on her way to cancer treatment. But it can also be celebratory when it captures your teenage daughter's excitement, grinning ear to ear and whooping with pure joy, when she scores the winning soccer goal. The experience evokes your acknowledgment that you wouldn't have missed that moment for any material reward.

Too often we quickly turn away from the harsh bite of empathy because sometimes it is accompanied by a sense of guilt. The child in another time and place would summon a smile and perhaps a hug. But now, with a shaved head and looking frail, she both frightens us with her "different" appearance and evokes empathic pain.

It is simply human to seek to avoid prolonging the pain. But if you can take an additional moment to let your empathy fully process the experience, you will better understand what you see and why it affects you in that way. Those types of difficult experiences confirm that you are a caring human being with the personal courage to share another human being's pain. This very positive observation about yourself is just one small way that empathy contributes to a more fulfilled life.

Awareness allows you to see your world more clearly. As a result, you open your heart (actually your brain's amygdala) to the plight of others and, therefore, to your empathy. This is where the magic resides. Empathy clears out the underbrush of moral ambivalence: *This is me they are ridiculing, not just some stranger.* Or, *Now that I know how he feels, I better understand his actions.* Or, *Her problem is my problem.* Our mirror neurons remind us that no matter how different we might seem from others, we are all connected.

Biologist and animal behaviorist Frans de Waal, whom I've mentioned earlier, refers to the step that humans and some mammals take after feeling empathy as "perspective taking." I have simplified that to simply *perspective*, but it is de Waal's inspiration. Perspective falls between empathy and acting upon those feelings. You are walking past a city alley and see a man beating a woman and hear her screams. Your heart goes out to her, but do you intervene and put yourself at risk, walk on, or call the police? This is an important moment in which your empathy is screaming "do something" and your reason is counseling caution, perhaps even urging flight. (I acknowledge that this is a dramatic example, but I use it because it so vividly illustrates the importance of perspective.)

There is no simple, universal answer about what to do when your empathy calls for action, which is why this process of obtaining perspective is important for both our safety and the effectiveness of our action.

Of course, for most people the situation that evokes empathy is more prosaic than witnessing a mugging. *Do I stop to help the woman pick up the parcels she dropped on the sidewalk or keep walking so that I'm not late for my meeting? Surely, others nearby will help her?* Or, *My friend sounds awful, depressed—and has for some time now. Should I go over to her house and tell her directly that I worry she might harm herself, or should I mind my own business?*

In addition to keeping us safe and ensuring the effectiveness of our action, perspective also reminds us of what is most important: *I can afford a minute or two to help this person, and I will feel better about myself if I do.* That simple restatement of what in life is important to us is another gift of empathy that pays dividends for a lifetime.

A coworker just broke up with her boyfriend. How do you comfort her? Your neighbor is struggling to start his lawnmower. Should you help, or would that embarrass him? An elderly man is unsure what bus to take to get to his doctor's office. Will you risk missing your own bus if you take the time to help him find his? A rift has developed between you and your brother-in-law over politics. Do you become combative, ignore him, or try to understand his point of view?

The most difficult situations are often when your empathy reaches across tribal lines to someone very different from you in demographics or personal beliefs, and your tribal instinct shouts *danger*, while your empathy whispers: *I know just how he feels.*

Seeking perspective also allows you to consider which form of altruism is likely to best serve your empathic command that you *do something.* You see a heart-wrenching story about children maimed in the Syrian war. Should you give a contribution or take the next plane to Damascus? This is where a conversation with a respected friend or family member could help you find the perspective you need to make the best choice of action.

To the person whose advice you seek, you provide them with the opportunity to be altruistic in helping you find the perspective you need in sorting this moral dilemma. So, the exchange provides rewards to you both. Connecting with others is a common theme in the world of empathy.

Altruism—an act of selfless concern for others. Each day we have opportunities to act on our empathy, from the routine to the dramatic. I wrote this book about empathy not to suggest that everyone needs to be a hero. Rather, I was animated by the enormous difference that can be made by the accumulation of little acts of altruism by one person, one family, one community, and one nation—millions of acts prompted by our empathy.

I acknowledge that some definitions of altruism suggest that it must be totally pure of any self-interest, any reward in return. I equate this debate to "How many angels can dance on the head of a pin?" I believe that the more useful definition is: a generous act that is principally for the betterment of others, not for oneself.

If you give up your seat on the crowded subway car to an exhausted elderly woman, is that altruism? I believe that the answer is an unqualified yes—you have committed a selfless act of concern for another. Similarly, it is altruism when in heavy stop-and-go traffic you let in the car on the side street; or you take time out of a busy day to patiently listen to a coworker tearfully describe her son's learning problems; or you reach out to the shy, unpopular classmate and introduce yourself.

This approach to engaging and applying your empathy is not an immutable law, but rather my suggestion for a place to start. We all have our individual ways of doing things, and you should be respectful of what works for you. The important point is that we need to change how we see the world around us, be aware of tribal walls (including our own), and commit ourselves to employing deliberate awareness to understand where in our daily lives, or in the wider world, empathy is needed.

If you live your life deliberately aware of the world around you, the number of empathic tugs certainly grows. But if you are comfortable with your feelings of empathy and you have reasonably good perspective on the practical actions you might take, you can manage your empathy to enrich your own life as well as the lives of others. You will have reached a comfortable balance: one in which your heart is open to the struggles and triumphs of others and your reason guides you to take effective action when necessary.

Being deliberately aware of the world around you and striking the right balance between an open heart and managed altruism is not simple, and it takes practice. Nor will you always get the balance right.

At least once I got that balance very wrong.

I remember vividly, and with no small amount of regret, being unaware and leaving my empathy clueless. When my mother died a few years ago, her best friend (a divorced woman in her seventies with grown kids) took the loss hard. I had known this woman for years, even if I saw her only rarely, and was aware that she suffered from anxiety and occasional depression.

After my mother's death, that friend called me a few times, ostensibly to discuss the logistics of my mother's estate to which she was a beneficiary, but in retrospect she was crying out for help. If I had been more aware, listened more deliberately, and been more empathic to her situation, I would have picked up on the risk of her hurting herself. But I missed the signals; my empathy never got activated, and she took her life. It was a tragic lesson for me about the life-and-death importance of deliberate awareness.

I heard the words that my mother's friend was using, but I never became aware of what she was really saying. It is true that she never said the words *I am so anxious and depressed that I might take my life*. But if at the time I had been more aware of her world, I might have understood that while being indirect in her words, my mother's friend was in serious psychological pain. At that point, my empathy would have mirrored the true depth of her pain and demanded that I address it.

That sad episode motivated me to take a suicide prevention course, much of which was devoted to being aware of the feelings of people around you. I don't recall that the word *empathy* was ever mentioned in that course, but the trainers implicitly communicated that the key to suicide prevention was the awareness of the pain in others—the empathy to understand why at-risk people feel as they do and the trained perspective to make the most effective intervention.

While I might wish otherwise, there is no simple mantra for tuning your empathy, and what I suggest in this book is not intended to serve as some pat self-improvement formula. My hope is that when the conflict and divisiveness we see around us seems more than we can bear, we will be reminded that we have each been endowed with an extraordinary resource that can break through barriers and bridge differences.

Imagine the impact on the entire world if just one in four people used deliberate awareness to see more clearly the world around them, to feel what others are feeling, and then, rather than return to their smartphones, they engaged in some way with a stranger, an adversary, the shy kid, the woman wearing the hijab, or the man shouting hateful slogans. It requires just a smile or a "good morning," or "Can I help you?" or "Have you been introduced to our team yet?" or "Do you have a place to sleep tonight?" Simple, simple, simple.

A skeptic would be justified in asking: Do little acts of kindness really make a difference? Will they change the arc of humanity? I don't know. However, what I think we all know anecdotally is that when someone goes out of their way for us, in even just a small way, it can bring a smile and a softening of our demeanor. And if we take notice when that happens, we will discover that, more often than not, we will "pay it forward." Our own personal experiences support the science that suggests empathy is contagious. Remember Lesbos.

As I complete the final rewrites of this book, I am interrupted by the news of two more mass shootings—one in Boulder, Colorado, in which ten died, and one just north of Atlanta in which eight lives were lost. Surely the reasons for these shootings will prove complex and the solutions even more so. Nevertheless, I only wish that some family members, neighbors, or friends had been more deliberately aware of the pain and confusion that the two troubled shooters surely felt, the empathy to understand that it could lead to violence, and the brave altruism to alert the police or health care officials.

Beyond these two dramatic events, imagine, day after day, simple examples of empathy growing in number, becoming contagious, and leading to even greater altruism. Perhaps these acts of empathy will eventually become the norm, while the "old days" of divisiveness and indifference gradually become denormalized like smoking in public spaces.

There is nothing in the lessons of evolution or biology, nor anything in neuroscience to suggest that our primordial fear of difference or instinct for retreat to tribal exclusion is destined to last forever. When experience proves that understanding the other person and connecting with her is more useful than retreating to the perceived safety of our tribes, social norms will establish empathy as the dominant behavior, and all of humanity will benefit.

Chapter Ten

Bridging the Divide

Moreover, I am cognizant of the interrelatedness of all
communities and states....We are all caught in an inescapable
network of mutuality, tied in a single garment of destiny.
Whatever affects one directly, affects all indirectly.
—Martin Luther King Jr.[1]

D r. King's quote just about sums it up.

We are all connected to one another and share the same destiny. Even the small things that we do, and don't do, as individuals affect all of humanity. Dr. King understood how this idea of connectedness worked; a single individual using racist language could establish a social norm of hate within his family. But in the 1960s, understanding how that individual act could impact the wider world took vision. King had that vision, but most people do not.

However, in our rapidly shrinking world of the twenty-first century, our connectedness is more literal and harder to deny. If I buy a gas guzzler vehicle that exacerbates climate change, the entire world feels the effects. Or if I post a tweet making fun of an overweight coworker, it could go viral and hurt thousands of others. We must not forget that the white supremacist who killed fifty worshippers in a New Zealand mosque was inspired by a white supremacist across the world in Norway. While Dr. King might not have lived to see the birth of the internet, the World

---

1   Martin Luther King Jr., "Letter from a Birmingham Jail," April 16, 1963, African Studies Center, University of Pennsylvania, https://www.africa.upenn.edu/Articles_Gen/Letter _Birmingham.html.

Wide Web made undeniable what he meant by "We are all caught in an inescapable network of mutuality."

Connectedness is potentially an enormous blessing; it can break down perceived differences, permit the sharing of lifesaving technology, and give all of us a sense that we belong to a global community of people who share much in common.

But for some, connectedness can mean "too close for comfort," as the demonstrations against global migration suggest. To many climate change deniers and Brexit advocates, global connectedness can mean intrusive, unwelcome change and new responsibilities.

Nevertheless, to paraphrase a wonderful line from the child's game of hide-and-seek: *Ready or not, here it comes.* Like it or not, our world is profoundly more connected than it was even a generation ago, and with accelerating new technology, it is only going to become more so.

The challenge before humanity is now quite stark: embrace this growing connectedness, manage our fears, and harvest the benefits that accrue from better *understanding* and social collaboration; or let fear and bias dictate, retreat to our tribal fortresses, and prepare for a modern Dark Age. These words are dramatic, but the truth about humanity's situation today is no less so.

In the paragraph above, I have highlighted the word *understanding* because it is the key to managing the fear of global connectedness. Which brings us back to the interplay of fear and empathy. A principal by-product of empathy is understanding, without which we are lost.

Fortunately, it would appear that empathy evolved to do exactly the job at hand. It puts us in the other's shoes, to feel what they feel and to begin to understand who they are, why they believe what they believe, why they do what they do, and where our common interests lie.

I have acknowledged throughout this book that empathy alone cannot resolve all of the conflicts and divisions in our world today. I have endeavored to avoid understating the complexity of the problems we face or overstating the specific role empathy might play in their resolution.

Nevertheless, my journey to better understand the growing divisiveness in America and around the world concluded with my conviction that empathy, organized on a global scale, could play a unique and pivotal role in guiding humanity toward a more peaceful and caring world.

As I have suggested, empathy can do even more than just prompt altruistic gestures toward those among us that are in pain or in need. It can provide the foundational understanding of "the other person," so essential to bridging between political parties, religions, ethnicities, genders, and cultures. The capacity to understand what the other person is feeling is crucial to bridge-building.

I understand the inevitable skepticism that these sweeping statements encourage. But that skepticism might diminish when one considers empathy's biologically strategic role in the development of human beings and its mechanism for activation: feeling what others feel.

The relentless intensity of human divisiveness today and concomitant lack of understanding of the "other guy" calls us to consider that empathy may be a trait of destiny in the story of humankind.

In previous chapters I have focused on the growing threat of division and tribalism and how the nature of empathy makes it uniquely suited as a counterbalance. In this chapter I stick my neck out a bit further, imagining how empathy might be used to begin bridging the divide between "them and us" and what the future might look like in a more empathic world.

I have grounded my optimism in what humankind has learned from history, politics, and psychology over millennia. It is true that humanity has forever carried the evolutionary baggage of a fear of "others," which has been the genesis of much conflict, but we are also blessed with the capacity to feel for the casualties of those conflicts, to bind their wounds, and to seek better understanding of what led to that conflict.

These blessings reflect the presence of empathy. While this does not provide empirical proof that greater empathy can reduce global conflict, it may be enough to prompt more and more people to conclude it is worth a try. It's not as if we have a surfeit of successful alternative strategies. Further, empathy has a powerful enabler in the age of viral communications, where even a small number of committed individuals can launch a movement.

Later in this chapter, I suggest specific actions that both our political leaders and individual citizens can take to harness our collective empathy to calm today's pandemic of fear and promote better understanding in the pursuit of a better world.

The writer, philosopher, and historian Jeremy Rifkin wrote a tour de force on empathy. In *The Empathic Civilization*, he employs an impressive, multidisciplinary research approach that spans ancient time through today to support his view that humankind has forever been inexorably evolving, if slowly and unevenly, toward a more empathic world.

However, despite his confidence in the power of empathy, Rifkin describes its evolution as pitted against strong destructive human forces, including the exploitation of nature, resource competition, and tribal conflict. After all of his research and years agonizing over these issues, he leaves us with a jarring question: Can we reach global empathy in time to avoid a collapse of civilization and save the Earth?[2]

A couple of decades ago that question might have been viewed as excessively alarmist, even crazy. But today, if our eyes are open, we cannot escape the overwhelming preponderance of scientific evidence that climate change and the concomitant loss of millions of species that hold our ecosystem together, plus the inevitable conflicts that will follow, surely represent an existential threat to our world as we know it.

I share both Rifkin's awe of empathy and his concern as to whether humankind will seize reason's hand in time to restrain the power that could extinguish our species. It seems increasingly likely to be a close-run affair.

While the scope of the challenge might seem overwhelming, driving most people into varying states of denial, we can no longer ignore the growing tribal vitriol, which could close off our last best hopes to reverse course. In America and in much of the world, our political leaders shout past each other, radio and cable demagogues spin intentionally damaging conspiracy theories, differing views are labeled

---

2   Jeremy Rifkin, *The Empathic Civilization: The Race to Global Consciousness in a World in Crisis* (New York: J. P. Tarcher/Penguin, 2010), introduction.

"fake news," and compromise is too often considered treasonous. It seems that no one is listening, no one is learning. History suggests that this is a very dangerous state of things.

This extreme divisiveness isn't just offensive; it is causing real suffering for millions, distracting us from growing existential threats and adding a coarseness to our social and political comity. Most concerning, it costs us time.

In 2019, the extraordinarily popular television series *Game of Thrones* concluded its multiyear run. The narrative was set in a fabled European Middle Ages in which the known world's tribal nation-states and internal power centers continuously war with each other, distracting their attention from the greater danger, the sole existential threat to humankind: the zombies of the north. The zombie metaphor may have been plucked from the world of science fiction, but it is apt. As we squabble about religious, racial, ethnic, and cultural differences, that incessant conflict distracts us from addressing global warming, nuclear proliferation, or incubating pandemics.

Indulging our misguided fears and petty animosities comes at a very high price.

My study of the fear of difference and resurgence of tribalism led me on a path of inquiry from the ever-present, surface-level symptoms of division (political partisanship, economic class warfare, immigration) to a deeper level of motivation (religious rivalry, racial and ethnic bias); and finally, to the primal, biological traits that are progenitors of all these reactions (a fear of others, being left behind, and social disruption).

My research seemed to continually lead me back to the same conclusion: it is this deep primal fear that triggers an instinct to gather in protective tribes, cast out the strangers, and resist counterevidence. The hot, molten core of conflict.

At the same time, we have learned from both our human biology and behavior over thousands of years that we need connection and cooperation to survive as a species. Longitudinal research studies (the same set of questions with the same subjects explored over decades) have shown that connection with others is the critical ingredient to individual fulfillment over a lifetime.

In retrospect, one of the most consequential societal oversights of the past century has been the lack of meaningful awareness of the long-term cultural and economic impact of recent, transformative technology, including the seismic waves of change that followed in its wake. This change both enriches and impoverishes the lives of millions, placing enormous stress on civilization's connective tissue.

The elites and well-to-do of nearly every developed industrial and postindustrial society—North America, Europe, much of Asia, South America, and increasingly Africa—have reveled in the seemingly boundless riches of a modern, technologically advanced global society, seemingly unaware or unconcerned that not everyone has shared in this bounty. Nor as a society did we anticipate the enormous economic and cultural upheaval that would spring from that disparity.

As I have suggested earlier, the economic and technological miracle of our post–World War II world entranced many of us with smartphones, superfast computers, the internet, and products from nearly anywhere in the world delivered to our door the next day. For millions of others, too often this miracle meant a loss of employment and damage to their sense of self-worth as others soared past them.

For America's poor and many people of color, this technological change has bypassed them, leaving behind internet deserts, healthy food deserts, and education deserts. The rapid technological advancements of the past few decades lit up much of America and produced enormous wealth for the fortunate few while leaving many behind with limited and often declining economic opportunity.

For others, this accelerating change also appeared to threaten the values and traditions that had for generations been their bedrock of security and opportunity: *work hard and be loyal and you have a job for life; my children will do better than I did; the majority of my fellow citizens look like me and worship my God; a high school education is a passport to the middle class.* This rapid change in social norms, and in the contract between the government and the governed, is one reason why many experts refer to this conflict as a "culture war."

It seems as if one-half of the world is saying, "Let's go! Faster, faster." while the other half is desperately screaming, "Stop! This is destroying all that I hold dear." This clash of fundamentally different perceptions of the road ahead takes many forms, from an angry political climate in many democracies, to the rise of autocratic leaders stifling divergent views, to the violence of the religious fundamentalists of ISIS, al-Qaeda, al-Shabaab, and Boko Haram.

Common to all of these divisions, whether relatively mild or extreme, is a near desperate attempt on one side to stop these forces of change, while on the other side resides an often unreflective conviction that this opposition to change is ignorant, misguided, or malevolent.

From these two global perspectives—modernity versus the more familiar or traditional—thousands of tribes have formed to give voice to a multitude of fears. In America alone, those fears span the gamut from real and imminent to the fodder of conspiracy theories: loss of employment, the adoption of Sharia law, whites becoming a minority, loss of sovereignty to international governments, destruction of America's heritage, loss of regional and local traditions, and the growing absence of religion from daily life. And this is a woefully incomplete list.

Perhaps it was inevitable that these fault lines, running across the very foundations of everyday life, would lead to intense, existential conflict—who we are, what we believe, and what we hold dear.

It soon became impossible for the world to ignore the growing confrontation. A new generation raised in a media-energized new world marched against its leaders from Egypt to Hong Kong. Demonstrators for a freer internet marched right past those calling for the enactment of Sharia law. The more radical one side got, the more extreme the other side.

Unfortunately, most of our world leaders view these tribal conflicts as disconnected from each other, as if they were just coincidental outbreaks of anger and violence. As a result, they have been playing a geopolitical game of whack-a-mole—fighting terrorism, ignoring the arguments of those who oppose globalism, appeasing a rash of autocratic leaders, halfheartedly addressing economic inequality, and on and on. Always addressing symptoms, not causes, and usually with a muddled response.

In most democracies there is a long list of political variables that lead to the election or defeat of one candidate over another, particularly in a close race like America's 2016 presidential election. In that race, Hillary Clinton would have won the electoral vote (in addition to the popular vote) and the presidency if she had done just marginally better with any of a dozen constituencies: millennials, white women, college-educated men, and others.

Nevertheless, the polling data is pretty clear that prominent among those missed opportunities (particularly because of their key geographic location in a few swing states) were economically dislocated and socially marginalized American workers. This was a constituency that for generations has voted for the Democrat at the top of the ticket.[3]

Secretary Clinton's campaign team seemed late to the realization that those blue-collar voters in Ohio, Michigan, and Wisconsin were so alienated and so angry that they would not only vote for a Republican but also one who represented everything that Democrats had for decades come to distrust. So, one revealing way to look at the 2016 election results is that just 74,000 of those former Democratic voters in three states determined the outcome of the election.

But of course, the election results reflected far more than just the story of 74,000 disgruntled Americans. That election, plus the vote in Great Britain to leave the European Union, were seismic political events, long in the making. Yet most of our elected leaders, of all parties, are still scrambling to figure out what all that shaking was about.

Interestingly, these alienated American voters were not particularly ideological. Twenty-four percent of Trump voters didn't know whether Democrats or Republicans were the more conservative, but they were desperate for someone in a position of power to understand their pain and to commit to helping them.[4]

---

3   See Global Strategy Group and Garin Hart Yang, "Post-Election Research: Persuadable and Drop-off Voters," *Washington Post*, April 2017, https://www.washingtonpost.com/r/2010-2019/WashingtonPost/2017/05/01/Editorial-Opinion/Graphics/Post-election_Research_Deck.pdf.

4   See the American National Election Studies report discussed in "A Special Report on Donald Trump's America," *The Economist*, July 1, 2017, https://www.economist.com/special-report/2017/06/29/a-special-report-on-donald-trumps-america.

Most observers on both sides of the political divide were surprised that after Donald Trump had been in office for two years the members of this tribe of angry, dislocated American workers remained deeply loyal to him, despite his lack of success in bringing jobs back to America, draining the swamp, or otherwise improving the lives of those dispossessed.

The pollsters and political pundits were once again confounded by the same phenomenon. They found the continued loyalty of Trump's core supporters bewildering. These voters were so alienated that they kept their eye on the big picture: Trump might fail to build a wall or pass better health care, but they held desperately tight to his central pledge to someday return America to a time when their economic, physical, and cultural security seemed assured.

Despite losing reelection in 2020, Donald Trump still won the support of 74 million American voters, a record only surpassed by Joe Biden's 81 million.

No doubt, some of Donald Trump's core supporters remained loyal out of a sense that they had no other option, with that conclusion confirmed by their perceptual and confirmation bias. Reflecting their own biases, most critics of Trump's supporters attribute their "blind loyalty" to ignorance or obstinacy, not to injustice, despair, and declining social status.

As a society we still have much to learn about our fellow Americans.

Donald Trump's election, the passage of Brexit, and the rise of ideologically extreme, populist candidates in Europe demonstrate that when expropriated by skillful demagogues, this fear can become a major destabilizing force within democracies. Again, it is not party or ideology that matters most to these populist voters; it is intensely felt emotional concerns about a changing world.

Despite a series of political and social shock waves from this accelerating change, most of our political leaders appear to have learned very little about the origins of the conflict and why those in opposing tribes are locked into self-defeating actions and reactions.

The conventional wisdom on the causes of this clash of ideas and beliefs is either too self-serving or from only a single perspective (unfair media, religious blasphemy, un-American beliefs) or too narrow in scope (echo chamber media, limited education, self-interest), or the "insight" is strictly about symptoms, not causes of the problems (radicalization, unemployment, economic inequality).

True, these symptoms are real and contribute to the destructiveness of the underlying disease and help perpetuate the strong feelings that we see in others and sometimes feel in ourselves. We show symptoms of this disease in seemingly innocuous comments like these: "Their shouts at the rallies are sexist or racist." "They don't know what they are talking about." "They all had smartphones; they couldn't be suffering too much." "Kneeling during the playing of our national anthem disrespects our nation and the flag."

As I have noted in different ways throughout this book, until we find the capacity to set aside our fear and anger about what the other tribe represents, we are no closer to reducing tribal conflict. Our quick dismissal of those with whom we disagree short-circuits our empathy, which is designed to shift the dialogue from "These people make no sense; they're crazy" to "These people seem so upset, I need to learn why they feel that way."

This desire for greater understanding of the other tribe might seem like a very small step forward in reducing tribal conflict, but this shift from being dismissive of our adversary to interested in the origin of their feelings is a giant leap forward in breaking the tribal dynamic.

Without an empathic insight into the pain or fear that "others" feel, understanding is sidelined and accommodation is made moot. Yet from Beijing to Istanbul to London to Washington, governments and their leadership seem deaf to the systemic forces creating so much suffering and protest. This lack of awareness and empathic understanding promises to continue this downward spiral of self-defeating action and reaction.

So how do we break this self-destructive cycle? What steps can we each take to make a difference? Those steps must directly address the primary driver of this cycle, a deep primal fear of difference brought to the surface by disruptive and accelerating change.

Like COVID-19, this fear crosses national boundaries: global migration, worldwide competition for jobs, clashing cultures and values, religious animosities, internet-enabled terrorism, economic inequality, and technological disruption.

Further, we cannot be confused when these fears are often articulated obliquely with words like *the changing character of our nation, unfair trade agreements, identity politics, unsecure borders.* When we do the translation, we find that the progenitor of these complaints and their symptoms remains fear of difference, which arrives with change in employment, traditions, conventions, societal makeup, and self-image.

Donald Trump's campaign slogan, "Make America Great Again," was enormously effective because it promised to return America to a time when it seemed more familiar and comfortable and belonged to his core supporters. While other political candidates overlooked the breadth and depth of this fear, Donald Trump did not. He understood, at least at an intuitive level, how to translate that fear into political advantage, as have other rising demagogic leaders around the world: Vladimir Putin of Russia, Nigel Farage of the UK, Recep Tayyip Erdoğan of Turkey, János Áder of Hungary, and Rodrigo Duterte of the Philippines to name just a few.

It is an old strategy supersized by modern media.

In 2016 and 2017, right in the heart of Europe, much of this fear-mongering approach was also wielded by populist presidential candidates in France and Austria, Marine Le Pen and Norbert Hofer. While Le Pen and Hofer lost, and Brexit and Trump won, each of their campaigns intensified the divisions in their countries and beyond.

So if, as a society and a world community, we are to bridge these differences, we must be more aware of this fear in ourselves and others and call on our empathy to better understand the other person's reaction to that fear. We then must use our reason to determine the steps, large and small, that we can take to demonstrate that we care and want to help.

My suggestions that follow are divided between what our elected leaders can do and what private individuals can do. They are parallel, but they reflect the difference in responsibilities and capacities of government and individual citizens.

What Our Political Leaders Can Do

Most of the political leaders in America and Europe campaign on "bringing our country together," but in office they revert to existing political expediency, appeasing the base. We can no longer afford to give our national division just lip service. There are enormous challenges ahead, closing the gap on economic inequality, mitigating the causes of climate change, and establishing a national consensus on America's future direction. We cannot do any of this without far greater compromise, collaboration, and comity—effective democracies require it.

Further, in the same way that we could not restart our economy after the pandemic without mitigating the spread of COVID-19, we cannot bring our country together without mitigating the spread of the primal fear roiling this nation.

Therefore, while this book is not intended to be prescription for government action, I have cited illustrative examples of economic and social problems that the government must address to begin to reduce that fear and bring us together.

This is where our leaders must start, in understanding the depth and implications of this primal fear. To do so, our political leaders will need to listen and learn more, and demonstrate that they understand how their constituents feel at that deep, not always top-of-mind level, as well as the reasons for their frustration and anger. Only then can they begin to take meaningful steps to address the suspicion and distrust that underlies the divisiveness.

Further, with that new understanding, our political leaders must address the political environment that nurtures those fears. They must redefine the practice of politics in America and across the globe. That means rejecting the politics of division and practice the politics of inclusion, forging broad alliances that are built on compromise and accommodation. In America that means eschewing the fantasy that we are not divided between a Blue America and a Red America; instead, acknowledge the divisions, the forces driving those divisions, and take the politically difficult steps of defusing those forces that divide us.

It wasn't many decades ago when American foreign policy was viewed as largely nonpartisan; America's security issues were too important to use for partisan advantage. We need to find ways to cordon off from partisanship as much government responsibility as possible—emergency relief, veterans affairs, foreign service, Medicare/Medicaid, and so on.

To the surprise of many political observers, President Joe Biden has taken a number of bold initial steps to address the fear of economic disruption and falling behind felt by so many Americans through his enormous $1.9 trillion COVID relief bill and his plans for an equally large infrastructure bill. Even his often-used phrase "Help is on the way" underscores his intent to address fear and uncertainty, while his phrase "Lower the temperature" seems to be designed to reduce the divisiveness. Lastly, he often uses the word *empathy* and tries to model it in public.

This is a good start toward the first step: acknowledging our divisions and demonstrating that our government understands why people are suffering and the importance of addressing the root causes. But we have a long way to go, and many, many more Americans will need to do their part.

Second, whatever our personal views on immigration might be, in every country, this fear of "others" will not be quieted until each country has broadly perceived control of its borders *and* agreement on an immigration policy that is humane, just, and practical. That means the political parties working together to create policy that reflects economic and social considerations without abandoning our nation's proud heritage of providing a place of refuge while upholding human rights.

That is a very tall order, but it is also absolutely essential to addressing the fears that drive us apart. Specifically, I see no option other than to do the politically perilous work of hammering out an omnibus immigration bill that is humane, just, and practical. In addition to controlling access, any compromise that reduces tribal conflict on this central issue must also include humane treatment and equal application of the rule of law for asylum seekers and economic refugees.

It is certainly true that some leaders are less interested in solving the global migration challenge than using it for political advantage. But from years working in politics, I know that there are many more elected officials who want to find practical answers if they have the public's support. So individuals have a critical role to play, as I explain later in this chapter.

Third, in America and much of Europe, when you listen carefully to those who articulate a fear of falling behind economically, you hear the pain of feeling "left behind," and with that the loss of social status and recognition. *We built this country, and you are going to just toss us on the trash heap of the unemployed, underemployed, or underpaid?* (i.e., underappreciated, under-recognized, under-rewarded)

Economic inequality is an enormously complex problem, and I don't suggest that I have a magic answer. Inequality involves not just white Americans who have been laid off as globalization and new educational requirements ravaged their communities but also a disproportionate number of people of color who face not just economic barriers but racial, ethnic, and religious discrimination as well. To relieve the fear of being left behind, our political leaders need to fully acknowledge the validity of the feelings of both groups and begin a national discussion on how to close that opportunity gap.

If we want to address the fear of being left behind, we must make the political and financial investment necessary to not just restore but also redesign America's badly broken ladder of economic opportunity. Here, too, the COVID-19 experience provides guidance. It has revealed the patchwork nature of America's economic safety net, a source of enormous anxiety for millions of Americans.

This will require that both political parties work in good faith and that a major investment be made in practical solutions—such as a minimum income payment or a higher minimum wage, affordable advanced educations or training, lifetime learning, and ways to use an ambitious shift to sustainable energy to revive Rust Belt cities and rural towns. I cite these ideas merely as examples to reflect the enormous scope of what we must do to address the issues around which so much divisive fear festers, so that the millions of discouraged workers are restored as valued contributors to their communities and our nation.

The COVID relief bill was passed strictly along partisan lines; it garnered not one Republican vote. This is not an encouraging sign.

These ideas and legislative proposals have spawned much debate, which is just what democracies are designed to encourage. But that debate must be free of those who seek to use fear to exploit it.

Lastly, evolutionary fear of extreme social disruption has taken the form of growing animosity between young and old, rural and urban, tech immersed and slow adopters, diversity advocates and diversity suspicious. This captures the faceoff that I mentioned earlier between those who want social change to slow—to preserve traditional values and familiar norms—and those who want to hit the accelerator to reap the rewards of that "progress."

The role that our political leaders could play here is to use their offices to facilitate a national discussion of the fear that divides us, the breadth of ideas that are available to address those fears, plus how we can adapt to and benefit from that change while sustaining the best of our nation's traditions and heritage.

Whether you agree or not with the illustrative specifics above, I hope that you can see that our nation's leaders, and those of nearly every other developed nation, must start first with understanding the depth of the evolutionary fears that threaten our democracies and our humanity—and address them as seriously as Americans experience them.

What We Can Each Do as Individuals

For months I looked for simple answers to how we might bring people out of their tribes to solve this divisiveness and its underlying fears—perhaps a political ideology, a single ambitious government program, or an educational effort that would change people's minds and behavior. But as I have suggested earlier in this chapter, this tribal conflict will require a great deal of hard work by each of us over many years.

I noted above that the efforts of the new administration to create bipartisan support for legislation designed to address these enormous issues have to date not been successful. That is not terribly surprising, given the history of the past few decades, but it underscores the importance of what we must do as individuals.

The important steps that our political leaders can and must take to begin to reduce the conflict will never succeed without the full-throated support of millions of individual citizens/voters. This tribal conflict will require a great deal of hard work by each of us over many years.

This is one of those times in history when our nation's citizens must demonstrate initiative and personal courage by stepping across tribal lines—political, economic, religious, racial, gender based, and more. We need to demonstrate what empathic leadership looks like at the level of the individual if we are to make progress in reducing misunderstanding and distrust, and dissolve the political gridlock that has hobbled our democracy for several decades. We must seize the leadership.

For example, citizens in countries around the world have begged nations and international organizations for decades to do something about the 100 million undetonated land mines in 60 countries that remained buried in fields and school yards—the lethal residue of dozens of wars. Land mines kill or maim over 25,000 civilians every year, including far too many children looking for a place to play.

But the nations and their political leaders did nothing; banning land mines was fiercely opposed by nearly every major country, including America. So in 1991 one woman, Jody Williams, an American, decided that she would flip the leadership on this issue. She began organizing people around the world from her kitchen table, identifying organizations that treated the casualties and reached out to thousands of individuals affected by the lethal scourge. She proposed a sweeping international treaty banning the use of the weapon and requiring nations responsible to clean up the buried mines.

As the early proponents of the treaty often remarked, the challenge of getting virtually the entire world to agree on eliminating this savage and ubiquitous weapon, still very much in use, was daunting. But they kept after it a day at a time until, on December 3, 1997, the Mine Ban Treaty was signed by 122 countries in Oslo, Norway. Fittingly, that same year Williams and the organization she founded, the International Campaign to Ban Landmines, shared the Nobel Peace Prize. Williams moved the world from her kitchen table.

Williams did not describe her campaign in those terms, but when the political leadership failed to act, she harnessed her own empathy, and she called on the empathy of many others to save the lives and the limbs of thousands of children.

We cannot all be Jody Williams, but we can each begin to develop our own empathy and use it to enhance understanding, communications, and compromise in our own worlds. If we each just take small conscious steps in that direction, it will have an extraordinary ripple effect, with the people we reach—paying that courtesy forward to still others.

Empathy is the key. For decades citizens have been calling for reform in how law enforcement uses force against people of color. Blacks have understandably been outraged about this for generations. But white Americas, particularly government officials at the state and local level, have kicked that can down the road forever.

Then, on May 25, 2020, the video of white police officer Derek Chauvin kneeling on the neck of Black George Floyd, in an act of cruel domination, blasted through social media, awakening the empathy of millions of middle-class white Americans. The image was so personal and graphic that it set off the mirror neurons that put millions of Americans right in the shoes of George Floyd...and they poured into the street.

Certainly some people will choose to direct their empathy on a grand scale, as did Jody Williams and several of the other extraordinary people described earlier. Others will join protests in the street or volunteer their time. But what will also move our world are millions of small gestures that demonstrate that we feel the pain or fear of others, that we will listen and learn, and that we care enough to try to help. Over time, this will begin to dissolve tribal fear and hatred, and create the necessary climate for understanding and reconciliation.

These acts of empathic kindness are things we can each do, each day, to reduce the fear of others through better understanding of those different from us. It will also bring us enormous personal reward. I am continually surprised at the reaction of people to whom I show even the smallest gestures of empathy. Commiserating with the grocery store cashier on her tough day; asking the overwhelmed nurse at urgent care how she is holding up; stopping to give directions to the foreign tourist who looks lost; volunteering my time to help new immigrants settle in. Simple.

The big smiles and clearly heartfelt "thank you so much" that I receive in return for these small gestures seem disproportionate to my effort. But it is because these public gestures of concern for strangers are so rare that they have so great an impact. That is one source of the power of small gestures of caring: they surprise and delight and contribute to setting a better tone between people.

Daily I work at trying to be more aware of the people around me and to interrupt the normal, frenetic pace of my day to act when that awareness identifies someone who could use my help or understanding. I disappoint myself when I fail to act, but I keep trying. I do this because I believe that if I am more aware and act on my empathy, it will represent a small but important contribution to creating a more humane, less adversarial world. I also do it because it makes my life more meaningful, and apparently, science supports this view.

One study of 397 American adults, through an initial survey and follow-ups, was designed to determine whether there was a measurable difference between happiness and meaningfulness. Actions that were found to be meaningful had a high correlation to happiness but not vice versa. Meaningfulness was more difficult to achieve than happiness. For example, being able to buy things correlated very strongly with happiness but not meaningfulness.

Giving to others and developing social relations (being connected to people) were among the handful of key actions that built a sense of meaningfulness. This notion of meaningfulness may be limited to humans (research is underway), but it is an essential ingredient to each of us living fulfilled lives as human beings.[5]

So, working to develop our empathy and acting altruistically isn't all work and no reward. Connecting with others and giving to others advance humanity in small ways and add meaning to our lives in a big way.

In the previous chapter, I suggested that empathy can serve as the first step in bridging this divide. We can do that by using our empathy to understand the other person and our altruism to help them understand us—the critical span that bridges the divide between us.

Of course, we can also demand that our political leaders search for their own empathy and understanding for the other tribe, seek honest dialogue, compromise, and work to eliminate the existing hyper-partisanship. This would be a seismic change. Most of the constituent correspondence that our political leaders receive today takes the form of a demand (sometimes even threats) that they resist any entreaties for compromise with the other party.

Frankly, in America and most developed countries, the very citizens who decry the political divisiveness are many of the same people who are driving it. We have some serious soul-searching to do if we truly want to break out of this prison of zero-sum tribal distrust and rivalry: "We win only if they lose." That must change to "We can all win if we work together."

The problem doesn't lie with "the other guy"—it lies with all of us, each of us. Accordingly, the solution requires changed behavior by each of us. I am suggesting that to find our way out of this maze we need to find our own empathy for "the other side" and begin to build bridges.

By using empathy to better understand ourselves and others, improving our listening and finding some agreement, we can create a powerful but simple personal action plan for bridging the divides we see every day.

---

5   Roy F. Baumeister, Kathleen D. Vohs, Jennifer Aaker, and Emily N. Garbinsky, "Some Key Differences between a Happy Life and a Meaningful Life," *Journal of Positive Psychology* 8, no. 6 (2013): 505–16.

I have built upon the original four elements of finding our empathy described earlier to develop six specific steps that I believe will help each of us activate our empathy and bridge divisions in our communities and in the larger world.

1. **Understand our own fears and biases.** Identify those who make us fearful, uncomfortable, or angry: someone of a different ethnicity, race, culture, or sexual orientation; someone with a disability; or someone with very different political views. Only after facing our own fears and understanding why we are fearful can we be open to engaging and understanding the fears of those different from us. If our ultimate goal is to build bridges, we must understand where our own fears and biases block our path forward.

2. **Be deliberately aware of the world around us.** We need to be better observers, particularly of those who inhabit different tribes and those who need our help or understanding. Repeatedly, Nicholas Winton demonstrated that while others were oblivious to the human suffering that was underway before World War II began, he was aware. He saw the pain of those lost children, took the time to understand the cruel conundrum facing their parents, and looked past his comfortable life in London to walk in the tiny shoes of his 640 children. Deliberate awareness can save lives, including our own.

3. **Listen with conviction to those most difficult for us to hear.** These are the people whom we believe are "wrong," "misguided," or even of malevolent intent. Go beyond what they say to discover what they mean. In turning himself Black and traveling the South on segregated buses, John Howard Griffin found a unique way to listen and learn about race relations in America—breaking through the codes of false accommodation between southern Blacks and whites and learning about the fears and profound ignorance of each other that still existed despite over three hundred years of history. Sometimes we can use our empathy to give ourselves the gift

of patience, to listen to those with whom we strongly disagree, to hear them out. Listening and genuinely hearing what others are saying and feeling activates our empathy, which is the most direct route to understanding.

4. **Share our own feelings.** What do you fear, or what makes you feel uncomfortable along with those things that you hold dear, and why? Inherent in the power of Natalie Hampton's smartphone app Sit With Us was the exchange of feelings about being excluded from the group and about the personal insecurity that can be so damaging among adults as well as teenagers. Her app provided the discreet means for teenagers to break the chilling silence of social exclusion that so many young people endure. It was a small step toward a less divisive world but a very creative one, demonstrating the limitless opportunities we have to circumvent tribal walls.

5. **Find points of agreement, any points.** Something that was out of reach before might now be possible. Even if they are very small bits of agreement, they can serve as initial cables of trust so essential to bridge building. C. P. Ellis and Ann Atwater crossed a yawning gap between Blacks and whites in North Carolina on school integration during the high-tension civil rights years by finding agreement on the smallest subjects first and then establishing mutual trust to bridge the most difficult issues. This modest but persistent approach built the confidence that others could follow. This is leadership.

6. **Reach out, take action.** Direct our empathic feelings to give us the courage and inspiration to take action to bridge differences and to come to one's aid if necessary. Help someone better understand their "obnoxious" uncle Charlie, or consciously choose to invite to dinner people with whom you disagree politically or who are of a different race, religion, or ethnicity. The people of Lesbos not only saved many lives of desperate refugees landing on their tiny island, but they also learned that these refugees from foreign lands had the same hopes and dreams as they did. They embraced these "different"

people with a warmth and generosity that stands as an example to be emulated by the entire world. The people of Lesbos bridged tribal walls that lay at the heart of one of today's most contentious social and political conflicts.

I acknowledge that the idea that empathy can bring down long-fortified tribal walls might seem fanciful to some. But in truth, this is how we have resolved tribal conflict for millennia. The use of nonviolent action by Gandhi and King, the inspiration for the League of Nations and then the United Nations, and the public outcry in America and Europe to limit nuclear weapons are just a few examples of the power of our empathy to bring people together.

It is true that in the twenty-first century humanity faces enormous challenges: global migration, economic dislocation, climate change, and challenges to democracy worldwide. And these forces will inevitably change America in ways that are enormously alarming to many.

While these are the cards that we have been dealt, there is reason to be optimistic. Empathy's long biological history and physical mechanism within the human brain suggest that it is a central gift to humanity. It provides us with the capacity to rise above our fears, to put down the weapons of our own destruction, and create a world of greater understanding and caring for one another.

After a lifetime of believing that the great challenges facing humanity could only be solved with the concerted efforts of nation-states and other mighty organizations, I now believe our greatest opportunity lies with the unique responsibility and power of the individual. Fortunately we live in an age in which technology has immeasurably enhanced that power, including the power to bring other individuals together for the common good. The internet stands as a metaphor, demonstrating the power—good and bad—of decentralized, individualized power to move mountains, from creating overnight global pop stars to overturning autocratic governments.

Of course, it isn't the internet that has the real power; it is the action or inaction of individuals that moves the world. Further, the empathy that resides within each of us houses the code for directing the human race toward the light of connectedness and away from the darkness of our tribal instincts. That empathic code can lead us to better understand those that threaten us, to pull down the tribal walls that keep us apart, and to begin the healing process of building bridges to a more humane and peaceful world.

In this book, I have recounted stories of extraordinary altruism and everyday acts of empathy to remind us that within each of us resides the capacity to make the extraordinary possible—even to alter the arc of humanity. It is now up to us.

Acknowledgments

Winston Churchill described writing a book as a rich and demanding adventure, through which the writer is dragooned into a writing exercise that mutates from an amusement to a monster. I would not have survived this passage without the love, patience, and insightful suggestions of my wife, Sally; the professional tips and sage advice of my dear friend and author Phil Kenney; the good humor and creative insights of my friend and fellow optimist Jim Mitchell; and the encouragement of my long-standing colleague from politics, Les Francis, who "got it" from day one and served as my wingman until the monster was "flung to the public."

Bibliography

ABC News. "Hidden America: Don't Shoot, I Want to Grow Up." Information graphic. Accessed November 15, 2019, http://abcnews.go.com/Nightline/fullpage/chicago-gang-violence-numbers-17509042.

Adams, John. "Adams' Argument for the Defense: 3–4 December 1770." Founders Online, National Archives, https://founders.archives.gov/documents/Adams/05-03-02-0001-0004-0016.

Alderman, Liz. "Greek Villagers Rescued Migrants. Now They Are the Ones Suffering." *New York Times*, August 17, 2016. https://www.nytimes.com/2016/08/18/world/europe/greece-lesbos-refugees.html.

Angier, Natalie. "Empathy Unfolds Slowly in a Child." *New York Times*, May 9, 1995.

Appelbaum, Yoni. "Only I Can Fix It." *Atlantic*, July 21, 2016. https://www.theatlantic.com/politics/archive/2016/07/trump-rnc-speech-alone-fix-it/492557/.

Barber, William, and Jonathan Wilson-Hartgrove. "Rev. William Barber Is Building a New 'Moral Movement' to Reach People on Race." Interview by Charlayne Hunter-Gault. *PBS NewsHour*, June 23, 2017. https://www.pbs.org/newshour/show/rev-william-barber-building-new-moral-movement-reach-people-race.

Baumeister, Roy F., Kathleen D. Vohs, Jennifer Aaker, and Emily N. Garbinsky. "Some Key Differences between a Happy Life and a Meaningful Life." *Journal of Positive Psychology* 8, no. 6 (2013): 505–16.

Beck, Julie. "This Article Won't Change Your Mind." *Atlantic*, March 2017.

Beckett, Lois. "Armed Protesters Demonstrate against COVID-19 Lockdown at Michigan Capitol." Guardian, April 20, 2020. https://www.theguardian.com/us-news/2020/apr/30/michigan-protests-coronavirus-lockdown-armed-capitol.

———. "Most Victims of US Mass Shootings Are Black, Data Analysis Finds." Guardian, May 23, 2016. https://www.theguardian.com/us-news/2016/may/23/mass-shootings-tracker-analysis-us-gun-control-reddit.

Bernstein, Lenny. "What Makes Someone Donate a Kidney to a Stranger?" *Washington Post*, April 28, 2017. https://www.washingtonpost.com/news/to-your-health/wp/2017/04/28/what-makes-people-donate-a-kidney-to-a-stranger/.

Blake, Aaron. "Kellyanne Conway's Legacy: The 'Alternative Facts'-ification of the GOP." *Washington Post*, August 24, 2020. https://www.washingtonpost.com/politics/2020/08/24/kellyanne-conways-legacy-alternative-facts-ification-gop/.

Bloom, Paul. *Against Empathy: The Case for Rational Compassion.* New York: Ecco, 2016.

Boyd, Andrew. *Daily Afflictions: The Agony of Being Connected to Everything in the Universe.* New York: W. W. Norton, 2002.

Bzeek, Mohamed. "The Foster Father Who Cares When Terminally Ill Kids Have No One." Interview by Gayle Tzemach Lemmon. *PBS NewsHour*, February 24, 2017. https://www.pbs.org/newshour/show/foster-father-cares-terminally-ill-kids-no-one.

Calaprice, Alice, ed. *The Ultimate Quotable Einstein.* Princeton, NJ: Princeton University Press, 2013.

Chesterton, G. K. *The Scandal of Father Brown.* New York: Dodd, Mead, 1935.

de Waal, Frans. *The Age of Empathy: Nature's Lessons for a Kinder Society.* New York: Crown, 2009.

———. *The Bonobo and the Atheist: In Search of Humanism among the Primates.* New York: W. W. Norton, 2013.

———. *Primates and Philosophers: How Morality Evolved.* Princeton, NJ: Princeton University Press, 2009.

The Economist. "A Special Report on Donald Trump's America." July 1, 2017. https://www.economist.com/special-report/2017/06/29/a-special-report-on-donald-trumps-america.

Faulkner, William. *A Fable.* New York: Penguin Random House, 1954.

Finlay, Liza. "Turns Out Empathy Is Contagious." *HuffPost*, November 30, 2012. http://www.huffingtonpost.ca/liza-finlay /teaching-kids-empathy_b_2220570.html.

Friedman, Thomas. *Thank You for Being Late: An Optimist's Guide to Thriving in the Age of Accelerations.* New York: Farrar, Straus & Giroux, 2016.

Goleman, Daniel. "Researchers Trace Empathy's Roots to Infancy." *New York Times*, March 28, 1989.

Global Strategy Group and Garin Hart Yang. "Post-Election Research: Persuadable and Drop-off Voters." *Washington Post*, April 2017. https://www.washingtonpost.com/r/2010-2019/WashingtonPost /2017/05/01/Editorial-Opinion/Graphics/Post -election_Research_Deck.pdf.

Griffin, John Howard. *Black Like Me.* Boston: Houghton Mifflin, 1961.

Hampton, Natalie. "About Sit With Us, Inc. – A 501(c)(3) Organization." Sit With Us. Accessed September 2–6, 2019. http://sitwithus .io./#!/About.

Hawthorne, Nathaniel. *The Scarlet Letter: A Romance.* Boston: Ticknor and Fields, 1850.

Iacoboni, Marco. *Mirroring People: The New Science of How We Connect with Others.* New York: Farrar, Straus & Giroux, 2008.

Jerit, Jennifer, and Jason Barabas. "Partisan Perceptual Bias and the Information Environment." *Journal of Politics* 74, no. 3 (July 2012): 672–84. https://doi.org/10.1017/s0022381612000187.

Keysers, Christian. *The Empathic Brain: How the Discovery of Mirror Neurons Changes Our Understanding of Human Nature.* Social Brain Press, 2011.

King, Martin Luther, Jr. "Address." Cornell College, Mount Vernon, Iowa, October 15, 1962. http://news.cornellcollege.edu /dr-martin-luther-kings-visit-to-cornell-college/.

———. "Letter from a Birmingham Jail." April 16, 1963. African Studies Center, University of Pennsylvania. https://www.africa .upenn.edu/Articles_Gen/Letter_Birmingham.html.

King, Robert. "Meet the Man in the Middle of the 'Unite the Right' Rally." *Indianapolis Star*, August 12, 2017. https://www.indystar

.com/story/news/2017/08/12/unite-right-white-nationalist-rally
-charlottesville-erupts-violence/562095001/.

Knowledge@Wharton High School. "'Sit With Us' Creator Natalie
Hampton's Crusade to Help Bullied Teens Feel Included."
September 27, 2016. http://kwhs.wharton.upenn.edu/2016/09
/sit-us-creator-natalie-hamptons-crusade-help-bullied-teens
-feel-included/.

Knowles, Elizabeth, ed. *Oxford Dictionary of Modern Quotations.*
Oxford: Oxford University Press, 2007.

LeDoux, Joseph E. *The Emotional Brain: The Mysterious Underpinnings
of Emotional Life.* New York: Simon & Schuster, 1996.

Lee, Harper. *To Kill a Mockingbird.* New York: HarperCollins, 1960.

Lee, Jaimy. "Hydroxychloroquine, Touted by Trump, Associated
with Higher Risk of Death in Study." MarketWatch, May 22,
2020. https://www.marketwatch.com/story/hydroxychloroquine
-touted-by-trump-associated-with-higher-risk-of-death-in
-study-2020-05-22.

Lincoln, Abraham. "First Inaugural Address." March 4, 1861. Avalon
Project. http://avalon.law.yale.edu/19th_century/lincoln1.asp.

Macaya, Melissa, Mike Hayes, Fernando Alfonso III, Daniella
Diaz, Jessie Yeung, Steve George, Ivana Kottasová, and Nick
Thompson. "George Floyd Protests Spread Nationwide."
CNN. Last updated May 30, 2020. https://www.cnn.com/us
/live-news/george-floyd-protest-updates-05-28-20/index.html.

Mann, Brian. "Trump Supporter: 'He Called for Unity, I Never Saw
Obama Call for Unity.'" NPR, August 14, 2017. https://www
.npr.org/2017/08/14/543259485/trump-supporter-he-called
-for-unity-i-never-saw-obama-call-for-unity.

Mounk, Yascha, and Roberto Stefan Foa. "The Signs of Deconsolidation."
Journal of Democracy 28, no. 1 (2017): 5–16.

Nashashibi, Rami. "Rebuilding a Chicago Neighborhood by Forging
Connections to the Muslim Community." Interview by Jeffrey
Brown. *PBS NewsHour,* June 23, 2017. https://www.pbs.org
/newshour/show/rebuilding-chicago-neighborhood-forging
-connections-muslim-community.

National Gang Center. "Measuring the Extent of Gang Problems." Accessed November 3, 2019. https://www.nationalgangcenter .gov/survey-analysis/measuring-the-extent-of-gang-problems.

Palagi, Elisabetta, Ivan Norscia, and Elisa Demuru. "Yawn Contagion in Humans and Bonobos: Emotional Affinity Matters More than Species." *PeerJ* (August 2012). https://peerj.com/articles/519/.pg.1.

Pew Research Center. *Partisanship and Political Animosity in 2016.* June 22, 2016. https://www.pewresearch.org/politics/2016/06/22 /appendix-a-measures-and-scales/.

———. "Support for Same-Sex Marriage Grows, Even among Groups That Had Been Skeptical." June 26, 2017. http://www.people -press.org/2017/06/26/support-for-same-sex-marriage-grows -even-among-groups-that-had-been-skeptical/.

Psychology Today. "Motivated Reasoning." Accessed October 12, 2019. https://www.psychologytoday.com/basics/motivated-reasoning.

Putnam, Robert D. *Bowling Alone: The Collapse and Revival of American Community.* New York: Simon & Schuster, 2000.

Rifkin, Jeremy. *The Empathic Civilization: The Race to Global Consciousness in a World in Crisis.* New York: J. P. Tarcher/Penguin, 2010.

Singal, Jesse. "Why Empathy Is Bad." *New York Magazine*, December 28, 2016.

Smith, Ryan. Forthcoming article. International Institute for Counter-Terrorism (ICT). https://www.ict.org.il/ContentWorld.aspx ?ID=1#gsc.tab=0.

Sullivan, Bryan. "Fox News Faces Lawsuit for Calling COVID-19 a 'Hoax.'" *Forbes*, April 10, 2020. https://www.forbes.com/sites /legalentertainment/2020/04/10/covid-19-lawsuit-against-fox -news/?sh=14e6e37f5739.

Terkel, Studs. "C. P. Ellis, 'Why I Quit the Klan.'" In *American Dreams: Lost and Found.* New York: New Press, 1980. Thoreau, Henry David. *Walden; or, Life in the Woods.* Mount Vernon, NY: Peter Pauper Press, 1954.

Townsend, Lucy. "How Much Has the Ice Bucket Challenge Achieved?" *BBC News Magazine*, September 2, 2014. http:// www.bbc.com/news/magazine-29013707.

Tufekci, Zeynep. *Twitter and Tear Gas: The Power and Fragility of Networked Protest.* New Haven, CT: Yale University Press, 2017.

Vekaria, Kruti M., Kristin M. Brethel-Haurwitz, Elise M. Cardinale, Sarah A. Stoycos, and Abigail A. Marsh. "Social Discounting and Distance Perceptions in Costly Altruism." *Nature Human Behaviour* 1, no. 5 (2017). https://doi.org/10.1038/s41562-017-0100.

Wallace, Kelly. "What Your Baby Knows Might Freak You Out." CNN, February 14, 2014. http://www.cnn.com/2014/02/13/living/what-babies-know-anderson-cooper-parents/index.html.

Wasserman, David, and Ally Flinn. "Introducing the 2017 Cook Political Report Partisan Voter Index." April 7, 2017. https://cookpolitical.com/introducing-2017-cook-political-report-partisan-voter-index.

Winton, Barbara. *If It's Not Impossible...: The Life of Sir Nicholas Winton.* Leicester, UK: Troubador, 2014.

Women's Rights Organizers and Condé Nast. *Together We Rise: Behind the Scenes at the Protest Heard around the World.* New York: HarperCollins, 2018.

Worral, Simon. "Yes, Animals Think and Feel. Here's How We Know." *National Geographic,* July 15, 2015. https://news.nationalgeographic.com/2015/07/150714-animal-dog-thinking-feelings-brain-science/.

Yousafzai, Malala. *I Am Malala: How One Girl Stood Up for Education and Changed the World.* New York: Little, Brown, 2013.

CPSIA information can be obtained
at www.ICGtesting.com
Printed in the USA
LVHW011022310821
696548LV00008B/358